GOD STILL DELIVERS

Reimagining Counseling with the Centrality of God

DR. JEFFREY LEACH

Dr. Jeffrey Leach

Published by DCI Publishers

Miami, Florida

www.thediakonia.com

DEDICATION

To my children you keep me striving for the best life so that I may leave you a legacy of a fearless Faith

FOREWORD

Dr. Oliver R. Phillips

INTRODUCTION

Dr. Oliver Phillips

Dr. Jeffrey Leach is my friend! But, more than that, Jeffrey has distinguished himself as a churchman par excellence.

Dr. Jeffrey Leach is a consummate practitioner of family counseling therapy and holistic mental health.

My acquaintance with Jeffrey retreats me to my years as an executive in the Global Ministry Center of the Church of the Nazarene. On a few occasions I sought his wise counsel on behalf of Ethnic ministers who needed counsel because of a burnout in their ministries. The burden and intricacies of the pastoral profession are not immune from stress and the threat of premature retirement. I found in Jeffrey a ready resource for these families.

Because of Dr. Leach's expansive understanding of culture, he was able to offer to these families a theocentric methodology that was unparalleled in the midst of many other available options. His intellectual grounding, coupled with his passion for excellence in ministry, gave him ultimate license to engage these families with therapeutic sessions that were redemptive, rehabilitative, and definitely atypical for these times.

Dr. Leach, because of his own background, exhibits a rare mix of intellect, selfless caring for others, playfulness, creativity, wicked wit and strength in adversity.

"God Still Delivers" is an expose of the methodology that is foundational to Dr. Leach's therapeutic counseling. While thousands have been beneficiaries of Leach's sessions, I believe that this volume will prove to be invaluable to those who seek help, as well as students who aspire to enter this vocation.

I highly recommend a careful and deliberate reading of this book!

TABLE OF CONTENTS

INTRODUCTION

Let me set the foundation for the process where we will eventually come to the knowledge, a place in our lives, where we are knowledgeable with regard to defeat we suffer in our lives, the attacks that we have. Legitimate or illegitimate, we have attacks from the devil and he is no respecter of persons, so he goes about seeking to devour whom he may. His prime target is a vulnerable person. A person who somehow might be ignorant of their rights as a Christian, of their position in Christ Jesus, or just like Hosea said, people who perish because of a lack of knowledge. We have to set some groundwork and go from there.

Put it in your mind real early that this is not necessarily some demon-bashing, deliverance, devil-casting-out, stomping, spitting-on, crushing kind of parade, although that could happen. You have to understand that all the problems we face are not necessarily going to be of a demonic sort. People have genuine problems other than a spiritual dysfunction.

There is the cognitive and behavioral problem one may have that needs discipline. There is a real need for the crucifixion of the self-life. So often when the self-life is not crucified and we find ourselves addicted to habits and patterns, we say, "Come cast this devil out of me," and there is not a devil to be cast out. Rather there is a discipline to be had. So you have to understand, not everything that manifests itself is going to be some hideous old devil. There is a cognitive aspect of the mind that needs to be improved, and there are aspects of communication in terms of interpersonal relationships.

Two people may be in a relationship and one person may be dealing with their own "demons", for want of another word in terms of their dysfunction, and they are inside of a relationship. Now you have a personal dysfunction within the individual and you couple that with a communication problem along with the dysfunction in another person, and you have need for tremendous communication. That is another problem that may not be devilish nor demonic.

Therefore, as we go through, I want you to understand what I am trying to do is a balanced menu of mental, physical, social, and spiritual healing. We can not be one-sided and think that everything is the devil.

One of the things I really want to spend some time on as we go through, is the area of intrapsyche. Intrapsyche simply has to do with inutero experiences, in terms of people who were rejected in the womb, etc. Adoption is a tremendous area of intrapsyche problems. For a child who is given up, the origins of that in terms of a spiritual emphasis is rejection, for whatever reasons. Even if the reasons may be noble.

That is why the term is coined in the medical field "intrapsyche", because it has to do with a mind that is before the existence of natural time as we have come to know it and understand it. It has become more and more an area of tremendous concern for me and other practitioners in the area of inner healing, because a lot of problems, as you begin to do a little digging, will go right back to that being its source. Somebody was not wanted or planned for or there were certain dysfunctions within the family, there were abortions, or different things. I will deal with that as I come to it, but keep in mind this is the balancing of things I want to present.

Then, of course, there is this final area of just plain old, gut-wrenching demon deliverance. Usually when one is diagnosed with some terminal illness, it has probably been at work for some two or three years and when it manifests, it is not like it just began. It began two or three years ago. It was a silent killer.

Now the same can be said about an individual who suffers some measure of dysfunction and does not have coping skills. It happened over a period of time. God in His miraculous, wonder-working power can deliver someone right now on the spot, but that is at the prerogative of God based on the individual's need.

I am not negating miracles. What I am saying is that there is need for training, disciplining, and working out many areas in a person's life. What we are dealing with is something that sets our life up from here to eternity and there is need for a natural progression of understanding of what caused it, how it is being manifested now, how to get rid of it, and then how to walk free from it. That is what I want to do. As far as I am concerned, knowledge is freedom. The more you know, the freer you are going to be.

We are in several kinds of bondage simply because we do not know how to get out of it. We do not understand its ramifications and oftentimes, we do not understand what is working against us. We do know we have a problem and that is about the extent of our knowledge. That is admission, but beyond this, what do you do? Where do you go from here?

Let us develop an hypothesis here that God is not the problem. If we are to develop this hypothesis that God is not the problem, then in a relationship conjoined, God and man, if He is not the problem, and we are suffering dysfunctions, then obviously the problem belongs to us. If we accept or at least rationalize in our mind that the problem may lie within us, and if that is true, then let us go into our first segment, "Through the eyes of God," and see how He sees us.

In order for you to have a right disposition about yourself, you must understand where you fit in terms of God's great purpose. How does God look at me? Bear in mind, I want you to assume we are talking about a dysfunctional person who has a problem. How does God see me conjointly in a relationship with Him and He not being the problem?

My overall goal will be this: To show that Jesus must take His proper place as King and Lord in the lives of each believer. That is going to be a very primary objective to achieve here. If that is established in the life of the believer, they are on the road to victory.

1

HOW DOES GOD SEE US?

II Chronicles 16:9 has been my text position from which I spring: "For the eyes of the Lord range throughout the earth to strengthen those whose hearts are fully committed to him. You have done a foolish things, and from now you will be at war."

For all that I am saying, II Chronicles 16:9 becomes backup. The eyes of the Lord are upon those whose hearts are fixed toward him.

Do you have a little child? I did a long time ago, as long as he is in my presence, he would be one of the safest little kids that you could probably see. In my adult mind, I understand that he does not have the ability to discern danger, he does not have the ability to discern what is right or wrong, he does not possess the skill we have as adults, to rightly figure between things, and so when I am with him, wherever we are, my eyes are always fixed on him. I look out for him.

If he climbs up on high places, a table or the top of the piano, I reach out and say to him, "Son, please come down," You do not want to create a panic in those times, so you go almost begging and entreating, "Please, let daddy help you…now, come here!" My eyes are trained on him, so to speak.

The eyes of God are upon those whose hearts are set toward him. An experience with the Father is so deep and so real that He wants to look out for you. He wants to protect you from the pitfalls. He wants to reach out and say, "Son, come down from there." We know when we have gone into our "high places." When we have elevated ourselves into mental positions of haughtiness and we have ascended into our high places, God wants to reach out and say, "Son, come down from there."

At the core of all our problems, as you look to a victorious Cristian warfare, you will find that ninety percent of the maladies we will be facing or dealing with, is because of result of ourselves going into those high places.

II Chronicles 16:9 says,

"…but you have done a foolish thing, and because you have done this things, you will be at war."

My overall goal in this text is that Jesus would take His proper place as Lord and King in each of our lives.

Colossians 2:9-12 reads,

"For in Christ all the fullness of the Deity lives in bodily form, and you have been given fullness in Christ, who is the head over every power and authority. In Him, you were also circumcised in the putting off of the sinful nature. Not with the circumcision done by Christ,

having been buried with Him in baptism and raised with Him through your faith and the power of God who raised Him from the dead."

We are the fullness of God in Christ Jesus. I want to discuss seeing from God's viewpoint. In other words, see this the way God is seeing it.

AWESOME GOD!

We have established beyond a reasonable doubt that God is omnipotent. He is governor, He is sustainer, He is creator of the universe, He holds all things in place, and He does not lose sleep doing it. God is an awesome God! He is provider, He is Yahweh, Tsidkenu...you can call all the names of God and in every respect, you would find that God is ultimately beyond the reaches of mere man or the devil.

God is in a class by Himself – infinite in wisdom, in mercy, in knowledge. God is just so awesome, I cannot begin to tell you in the economy of the English language how awesome God is, how mighty God is, and how praiseworthy God is! God is a big, great, wonderful God!

Now take this into consideration. This great infinite mind of God sat down one day in the heavens and decided, because He is so good and because He is so tremendous, that He was going to produce something with the caliber and nature expressly ordered to fit God's desire. I think He might have stormed around the heavens for a while in the presence of the Son and the Spirit, and the light went on, and the wisdom and intellect of God in His infiniteness and His perfectness, God said He wanted something to express what His mind could conceive, what was inside of Him, the depth of His creativity, and all He could think about was to make person like you. You are the sum total of the ultimate expression of the mind of God in His fullest creative potential. God could not find anything nobler, bigger, better, more wonderful than to create His masterpiece, His work…man…YOU!

If you understand this like I think I am understanding it, demons would run because I am the apple of His eye! God loves me! I do not love me like God loves me. God really loves me! Knowing this should change our thinking and revolutionize our life. God, as brilliant as He is, came up with man. This is it. From God's point of view, yes, this is it – you. For this reason, we are made in the image of God.

IN THE IMAGE OF GOD

What is the image of God? We have looked at the infiniteness of His creativity. What is His image therefore because of this creativity? Is it that I am tall, dark, and handsome? Is that the image of God?

I was talking to a small child some time back. I had her in my lap and we were chatting, having a wonderful conversation, and then she looked into my face and was kind of overcome with my appearance. As she gazed with great intent into my face, she reached up and touched my skin and said, "You got mud all over your skin." Her interpretation of me being black, she was only four years old.

Is this the image of God. Is it because my skin is "Covered with mud?" Is it because I am 6'2-1/2? Is it because I am about 280 poundish? Is it because you are tall, muscular, blond, and good-looking? Is that the image of God? No. The image of God is the ability in the believer to choose between alternatives, what is right as opposed to what is wrong.

When God sees you in His image, He sees a person who is able to make choices. Choices that reflect the nature of Christ in the believer. In other words, the true image of a believer is a replication, a duplication of the lifestyle of Jesus Christ.

That is how you have the image...you mirror the life of Christ in you. It has nothing to do with white or black, tall or short, fat or skinny. None of these things matter.

God sees you in His image as an individual who knows how to choose right. It is your choices that ultimately cause you to ascend the spiritual scale. Poor choices will leave you vulnerable to the attacks of the enemy. Good choices will cause you to walk in the land of milk and honey. So the formation of God's image as He sees you, how God wants to see you presently, is a man, woman, boy, or girl who knows how to choose discriminately between sin and right.

That is the image of God.

IDOLATRY LEADS TO DECEPTION

Ezekiel 14:1-11 says,

"Some of the elders of Israel came to me and sat down in front of me. Then the word of the Lord came to me. Son of man, these men have set up idols in their hearts and put wicked stumbling blocks before their faces. Should I let them inquire of Me at all? Therefore, speak to them and tell them, this is what the sovereign Lord says. When any Israelite sets up idols in his heart and puts a wicked stumbling block before his face, and then goes to a prophet, I, the Lord, will answer him myself in keeping with his great idolatry. I will do this to recapture the hearts of

the people of Israel who have all deserted me for their idols. Therefore, say to the house of Israel, this is what the sovereign Lord says, 'Repent. Turn from your idols and renounce all your detestable practices. When any Israelite or any alien living in Israel separates himself from Me and sets up idols in his heart and puts a wicked stumbling block before his face, and then goes to a prophet to inquire of Me, I, the Lord, will answer him Myself. I will set My face against that man and make him an example and a byword. I will cut him off from my People, and then you will know that I am the Lord. And if the prophet is enticed utter a prophecy, I the Lord have enticed that prophet and I will stretch out My hand against him and destroy him from among My people, Israel. They will bare their guilt. The prophet will be as guilty as the one who consults him. Then the people of Israel will no longer stray from Me, nor will they defile themselves anymore with all their sins. They will be My people, and I will be their God,' declares the sovereign Lord."[3]

See how God is seeing us. What we have to take into consideration here is that as they had gone wrong or felt like they had drifted away from God and lost that intimacy with God, the first thing they did was run to the prophet. "Give us a word. Please give us a word." If we live clean before God, we won't have to run to the prophet to give us a word.

People who seek the prophet are uncertain about their own spirituality. They are uncertain about their directions. They have lost intimacy with God. Mind you, I am not cutting down the prophet. Don't get me wrong. Oh how, we need a revival of that ministry. I am talking about those who callously live their lives and hope that occasionally they will take some directions from the prophet. So they go along any way they want and then…(prophet check), so they might turn left or right. They continue to check with the prophet for the way to go.

God says, "Because of your idols, I will cause that prophet to lie to you." He said, "I will entice that man to give you word." A better translation would be, "I will cause that man to lie to you. Because you want to hear something, I will make him lie to you. I will let him tell you just what you want to hear, and then I am going to hold you and him accountable. Both you and the lying prophet I will hold accountable."

Get rid of the idols. Pull down the high places and there will be no need for a prophet check. This is how God is seeing you in His image that He has for you. He wants relationship with you.

WORSHIP BUILDS RELATIONSHIP

Romans 12:1-2 reads,

> *"I beseech you therefore, brethren, by the mercies of God, that ye present your bodies a living sacrifice, holy, acceptable unto God, which is your reasonable service. And be not confirmed to this world: but be ye transformed by the renewing of your mind, that ye may prove what is that good, and acceptable, and perfect will of God."*[4]

What is God's desire? How is God seeing you? How does God want to see you? Holy and acceptable. There is a word in Hebrew, it is called "kodesh" – worship. He wants us sacrificially worshipping Him. The ultimate expectation on the part of God for the relationship is that we worship Him. If we worship God out of a deep sense of worship, we will have a revelatory experience with Him, and the Word of God will become manifest in our lives. We will know because we will discern by the Spirit a true interpretation of the will of God for us.

What is worship? Is it singing and dancing? Yes, it is that. Is it paying your tithes? Yes, it is that. Is it fellowship? It is that also, but beyond all of that, worship is truth in the innermost parts. No guile, no lies, no hypocrisy...deep juice that emerges like a river, flowing from your innermost being wherein you can tell God every detail about your life and your personality. When you feel hypocritical or feel a certain animosity for the brethren, you can tell Him. This is worship, this is intimacy, this is fellowship beyond description..."God, right now I would really, really rather Mike not speak to me, because that is how I feel. I know it is not right, but I am having these feelings inside me and I really want you to work with me, Lord. Let's worship, Lord, so you might show me how to love Mike and how to get above this hurdle and embrace him with truth, not hypocrisy. Not because it is socially nice or politically correct that I extend fellowship and greet him, not because it is the right church thing to do, but because truth comes from within my heart and says, because the Father loves me and I am unworthy, but He loves me in spite of this, I can love you too." This is worship.

RE-TRAINED TO BE SALT AND LIGHT

The soul needs to be retrained. A lack of knowledge of the Word causes the old ways to remain in ascendance. Hosea 4:6 says,

> *"My people are destroyed from lack of knowledge. Because you have rejected knowledge, I also reject you as My priests; because you have ignored the law of your God, I also will ignore your children."*[5]

Now you notice He didn't say you didn't know; He said that you ignored the law. You can only ignore something you are aware of. "My people perish for a lack of knowledge." Then it goes on to say, "They have ignored the law of God." Why are we having these defeats. Back up to Chronicles 16:9. "You have known truth and you have ignored truth. You have chosen to turn your back against truth so that you might allow yourselves to fulfill the lust of your flesh. When you ignore truth, it is simply because you are saying, "I want to do what I want to do!" This is a high place. You ignore the very truth of the Word of God, and because of it, you will perish.

I was tampering with a particular piece of equipment without first reading the instructions. It looked simple. Anybody with half a brain, the right side that is, could figure it out. This is one of those "macho" kind of things, you know, "I can fix that" I proceeded in my ignorance and lack of knowledge and my attention was drawn to the humongous amount of smoke coming out of it. I wasn't supposed to work that way.

When you have a familiarity with the Word of God that makes you think you are an expert, that is a high place. God said in His Word, "Study to show yourselves approved." Study...study...study to show yourselves approved. A workman not being ashamed, not being embarrassed by "the smoke" because you took things into your own hands. That is a high place. When people want to talk you about the scripture and you already know the answer...when they try to tell you something because it has really deposited into their spirit, but you have a better interpretation, that is a high place...high mindedness.

Proverbs 16:18 has this to say,

> *"Pride goeth before destruction, and a haughty spirit, before a fall."*[6]

It is a prideful spirit that assumes he knows it all. This is how God is seeing you. This is not how God wants to see you, but this is how God is seeing you. We need to have God's view of sin. We need to get His design for our life.

Matthew 5:13-16 says,

"You are the salt of the earth; but if the salt loses its saltiness, how can it be made salty again? It is no longer good for anything, except to be thrown out and trampled by men. You are the light of the world. A city on a hill cannot be hidden. Neither do people light a lamp and put it under a bowl. Instead they put it on its stand, and it gives light to everyone in the house. In the same way, let your light shine before men, that they many see your good deeds and praise your Father in heaven.

First you are the salt – you are to lend flavor to life. How do you define a sourpuss? Words cannot begin to define a sourpuss. You are supposed to lend flavor to life. You are supposed to salt the earth. If you lose that saltiness, you serve no real purpose. You are a light in a dark world.

Several years ago, I had a digital watch when they were new. It was cooler than ice! It cost around $300 for one. I came to the United States and they were about $10 a piece, but we were out there in Trinidad in the dark and we did not know any better, so we paid $300. My goodness, you could see me from a mile off. However, it taught me a very valuable lesson.

One day, I guess because I was so obnoxious and prideful, some guys decided to teach me a lesson in humility. I was on the production floor at my job, strutting around and watching them work, and I walked into the freezer room and they locked me in the ice room where it is 30 degrees. It was pitch black. I mean the darkest night you have ever dreamed of in your life…you couldn't see your hand if it were right on your nose…it was that dark. Then I heard the fans come on so the temperature began to go down even lower. A strange thing happened. I turned on my digital watch with the little neon light, and it pierced the darkness. It absolutely lit up that pitch black room. I found my way to the door and released myself by the light of that watch. That is how God wants to see us – as light in a dark place.

THE DEVIL DIDN'T MAKE ME DO IT

Sometimes new Christians, and not just new Christians, but a whole lot of people believe that every problem they have is because of the devil. Now I am not one for being easy on the devil, but sometimes he is innocent. That is a paradox in itself, the devil is innocent. That is a misnomer. Still, not everything can be attributed to him. Sometimes in this whole big thing about God seeing us and seeing ourselves from God's viewpoint, we have to understand we oftentimes take ourselves willfully out of the covering of God. Let me tell you how that happens.

When you are faced with a situation that may be considered a trial or temptation, one of the first things that happens to you is desire grows within you. I never saw a man who sinned without first having a desire. Desire leads to passion, passion leads to ruthless rage, and before you know it, you are overwhelmed. But when we are confronted with these situations, we must make a choice. Remember what the perfect image of God is? It is not in the outward appearance, but it is in the ability to choose right and make a perfect choice like Christ would.

When we are confronted with these kinds of situations and we find ourselves being overwhelmed to the point that we commit ourselves and our body follows our soul in an action of sin, there is something very intrinsic that takes place there. There is a deliberate, conscious effort on the part of the believer to dismiss the Spirit from their life. I challenge you to honestly refute, if you can, that you cannot sin until you dismiss the presence of the spirit from your being. You cannot proceed into an area of sin and sinful living unless you have first struck a compromise with the devil, become overwhelmed by him, and then finally choose to proceed in the sinful act. I guarantee the Spirit of God will stay by you and plead with you over and over and over again, saying, "This is the way. Walk ye in it and you will find rest for your soul."

I was studying negotiations and an interesting thing unfolded to me. Anytime you begin to negotiate, the foundation upon which negotiation stands is a word called compromise. When you negotiate, you have to compromise. When temptation comes and you begin to negotiate with the devil as to how much you can safety do and get away with, you will compromise, and compromise has got in it a dismissal of the Spirit. You have to release Him. You have to let Him go because he won't stay along and watch it. He won't be a part of it. The minute that you dismiss the Spirit of God from your life, you open the door.

This is what victorious Christian warfare is about. This is what Chronicles talks about. "You have done a foolish thing." You have opened the door in compromise and because you have opened the door, you will be at war with God and with the enemy of God.

I refer to Zechariah 1:18-21 that says,

"Then I looked up and there before me were four horns! I asked the angel who was speaking to me, 'What are these?' He answered me, "These are the horns that scattered Judah, Israel, and Jerusalem! Then the Lord showed me four craftsmen. I asked, "What are these coming to do?' He answered, "These are the horns that scattered Judah so that no one could raise his head, but the craftsmen have come to terrify them and throw down these horns of the nations who lifted up their horns against the land of Judah to scatter its people."

Who are these craftsmen? Who is the Lord of Hosts? Who is this great and might warrior? Who is he that is come to throw down the horns that have been set up? There is a plan in the kingdom of God, which as we know it is righteousness, joy, and peace in the Holy Ghost. There is a plan in the kingdom at work right now to take back the territory, to take back lost ground, to reclaim the cities, the citadels, to reclaim families, lives, marriages, homes, kids, and institutions.

I don't mean to drift off into politics, but there is a woman by the name of Attenbury. In the senate confirmation, she had her "personal friend," her companion who is of the same gender. This is a woman who put pressure on the Boy Scouts of America to cause them to lose funding through the United Way because they would not accept people who live alternate lifestyles, to be leaders of little boys. Our nation sat with such warmth and cordiality and recognized this as a standard of excellence and direction for our nation.

There is a spirit now at work in this country. Righteousness exalts a nation, but sin is reproach unto any people. All the Jezebels and Ahabs and all we have to deal with starts way up in Washington. Do you understand what we have to deal with? It has become rampant in our nation, but God has a plan to retake the city. I have a righteous anger about the moves and measures they are wanting to pass in our institutions in our land, legislation that they are trying to push that must make us hire people to teach our kids, even in Christian schools, and if we don't they will sue us and shut us down. God has a plan to retake this city. This nation was founded on God, and we have got to go back to God!

Got introduced the plan early on in Genesis 15. He created covenants. God's Word is His bond and He says in James 4:8,

"If you will draw nigh unto me, I will draw nigh unto you."[9]

As long as this law remains within you, as you mediate upon it, as you speak it forth from your lips and it stays within your heart, and you tie it on your door post, and on our head, and you put it upon your children, and so on and so forth, He will bless you.

Do you know what is a blessing is? A blessing is an endowment of power from on high. It is the releasing of the powers of the Godhead out upon His people. In this last day, He will pour out of His Spirit upon all flesh.

2

CAN A CHRISTIAN HAVE A DEMON?

II Chronicles 16:9,

"For the eyes of the Lord range throughout the earth to strengthen those whose hearts are fully committed to Him. You have done a foolish thing, and from now on you will be at war."[10]

Not the kind of stuff we want to hear… at least not the latter part of that verse anyway. The first part is really good. It is the blessings we like; it is the work that we cannot stand. The eyes of the Lord are upon us and ranging throughout the earth. He is for those who are fully committed to Him, and for those who are not fully committed to Him, they will eventually and without fear of contraction, find themselves at war.

The tragedy of this warfare is that they are at war with God and they are at war with the enemies of God, so for being foolish, they will get to be beaten up twice instead of once. We stand in the face the punitive measures of God for breaking His covenant, and a covenant breaker is a wounded, beaten-up person. Then we face the onslaught of the enemy because he sees us outside of God's territory and he decides we are good for demon food. To be out of focus in God is to have what we call a "double whammy"! We are dealing with God's wrath (not that He has purposed to have a wrath against us, but because of stepping out of the covering and the umbrella of God, we expose ourself to that natural consequence) and along with that, we expose ourself to the enemy who finds us a good target – good meat so to speak.

We are entering into spiritual warfare and I don't want for a moment, our eyes to get off track and into all kinds of demonology. This is not the focus. It is not the emphasis. I am not looking for a demon under every rock. There are all kinds of maladies that do not necessarily have spiritual overtones.

Some people have biochemical disorders. Some people eat the wrong kinds of food. There are all kinds of things that happen. Not everything is demonic and not everybody is demon-possessed, but a lot of people are, and so I pose my hypothesis on this premise: Can a Cristian have a demon?

We are trying to expose the works of the devil. We are trying to become over-comers. We are trying to understand where we may have gone wrong, how we may have opened doors, and how we may have left ourselves vulnerable.

I pose my thesis statement to you and I pray God we do not become offended or incited by some religious spirit that makes us offensive. What I am about to say can be construed offensive. For time immemorial there have been debates in theological circles and they will debate this issue until the Lord comes again. Can a Cristian have a demon? According to the Word of God, no...absolutely not. The Word does not state that a Christian can have a demon. It says believers can.

Yes, we can have a demon spirit. Yes, we can have an unclean spirit that afflicts and affects us in negative ways and produces all kinds of odd behaviors, all kinds of manifestations that make us the kind of person no one wants to be around.

THE THREE "R'S" FOR DEMON HABITATION

There are three basic areas within which we find the person, the individual, the believer who needs deliverance and needs to have the Spirit of God repair their life. These three basic areas are rejection, resentment, and rebellion.

Rejection comes first, It gives rise to resentment because we are wounded – our spirit is bruised – and so we begin to resent. As a result of resentment, there are host and multitudes of different maladies – anger, rage, temper, fits of jealousy, envy, murder, violence. From that proceeds rebellion.

Rebellion is willfully known transgression of the known will of God. One rebels when he is rejected, filled with resentment, and then he goes into rebellion, and those are entities that are demonic. These are areas that the believer is moved into – the soul is transported from a place of innocence into a place of condemnation, and what is at work here is a demonic entity that is creating manifestations within the life of the believer that is not necessarily controlled by God. He acts weird, uncontrollable, and he does things that almost make you want to say, "What a deluded person."

For all intent and purposes, we love that person and we know in our heart of hearts, the Spirit of God genuinely resides in that person's heart, unmistakably. Then why does he or she become a Jekyll and Hyde? Why is he ambivalent...one moment being sober and the next minute like he is high on crack? It is the influence of the demonic. It is not "that is the way I am," "this is the way I was born," "this is a trait that my grandfather handed down to me," "this is a generational thing." It is not a personality or character trait. It is a spiritual manifestation and, I daresay that to be so, because in all my experience in the area of counseling and deliverance, I cannot remember working with a non-Christian and casting a spirit out of them. I cannot remember ever going up to a sinner and slapping them across the head and saying, "Come out you foul spirit!"

I have always worked with Christian people, so part of my premise in my own experience is that, I believe those people to be Holy Ghost filled, blood washed, sanctified, born again, and yet their souls have become filled with an entity that drives them to limitless ends. Let us not get into a charismatic stupor and walk in ignorance and proclaim aloud that it does not happen and it does not exist.

SPIRITUAL HOUSE CLEANING

I am reminded of a scripture where Jesus cast out an evil spirit in a man. Now, if Jesus has anything to do with you, if He ever came your way and ministered to you, I consider you a believer. If you had an encounter with the Lord, I consider you a believer because I know my Jesus will not leave you unattended in your situation without filling your need. Jesus worked with the man, cast the demon out, and set him free. He has loosened and undone the heavy burdens, and He turns right over to the man and says, "You clean your house and you stay free because you are the believer. If you fail to do this, seven more demons worse than that one will come and refill you."

When a demon comes back, it comes back with previous knowledge of what happened before and a new divisive means as how to not be easily entrapped the second times, so he comes back with greater cunning. Watch out about how you walk. Watch out about how you keep your house clean. I believe ninety percent of our spiritual warfare will be accomplished and conquered when we know how to possess our vessels in honor and sanctification.

When you and I possess the ability through the knowledge of the Word of God, the abiding presence of the Word of God, richly implanted, imputed into our beings, we would have taken care of a lot of deliverance. Tell me scripturally if I don't have a sound position that within the body of believers, there is room…great room…and great leverage…and how we take great leverage in allowing unclean spirits to come into our being.

If we understand that half of the problem and half of the warfare has come to an end when we clean ourselves out from these unclean spirits, we would understand and we would have a better perspective of warfare and what we are all about. We are not supposed to blindly engage ourselves in confrontation with the devil until we first learn how to master the art of keeping ourselves clean. This is the emphasis with which I am beginning.

There is no where in the Bible where it expressly and explicitly says that a Christian can have a demon. There is scriptural ground, however, that states believer's can.

We can memorize all of the Bible and still go to hell memorizing the Bible. No part of this Bible is any good to us unless it is used. Head knowledge will not get us into Heaven – it takes heart knowledge. It take discernment. It takes the revelatory experience of the Word of God manifesting Himself in us in what we have come to know as a "rhema" word – a revealing Word of God. It is a word that comes to us and is manifested within our being, in such a sensory way that it revolutionizes our life and changes us forever. This is what we are after. A word that changes our life forever.

I searched my mind to find one incident in the last fifteen years where I had cast a demon out of some non Christian sinner or some ungodly person I met on the street. I can hardly think of many, not that there is not any of them ,my experience has been different primarily because I worked mainly within the church and in a Christian environment. Good, born-again, Christian people who have opened the doors in their lives and allowed the enemy to creep in unawares and finally take over their being causing them the affliction of being demonized.

WARNING SIGNALS

These are possible warnings signals that say we may possibly need to have an encounter with a deliverance worker or at least a counsellor to deal with demonization.

1. Confused or disordered thinking. Loss of touch with reality. Delusions. Persistence of erroneous convictions in the face of contrary evidence. We know the truth. It is staring us in the face. It will kick us in the behind, but yet we defy it. This is often called a religious spirit, but we will not call it that.

1) At one time, I was putting on a crusade overseas in a village and putting up a big tent that could seat a couple of thousand people, and all kinds of strange, demonic things started happening. Rain like you have never seen, started falling right where the tent was and no where else. The clouds were black, thunderous, and thick, and it was right where we were. A hurricane-like tornado wind came down right there and no where else. It ripped the tent up and tossed it about a hundred yards away into an open field, but it did not interfere with anything else. The powers were being shaken and there were a lot of people who did not like what was going on in the village. I was taking business away from them, I guess. I stood up and spoke up into the skies and said, "I will have this crusade. I will build this tent even if it kills me." Within two days I had spinal meningitis. The powers and entities that be, crept into my being through my confession. I opened a door through my mouth.

2) Obsessions. Absorption with a subject or idea to the exclusion of others. Compulsion. Uncontrollable urges. In my six hundred page manual, I discovered there is a spirit called "First Drink," especially to those who are going on the wagon. It creates an uncontrollable urge to repeat the performance. "First Drink" comes in because of a desire that rises above the knowledge of the Word of God, and anytime your desire rises above the knowledge of the Word of God, and anytime your desire rises above the knowledge of the truth of the Word of God, guess who is going to come in?

3) Inability to cope with minor problems with daily routine.

4) Difficulty in making a keeping friends. Poor social skills. Isolation. Withdrawal from society. A loner lifestyle.

5) A pattern of failure across the board – in school, at work, in sports, in personal relationships. These are obvious signs that you may need some help.

6) Prolonged or severe depression. Suicidal threats and suicide attempts. This thing in unleashed against the church today like we would never believe.

7) Immaturity. Infantile behavior such as bed-wetting, over-dependence on the mother, excessive clinging as a child, continuing dependence in the teens and even into the twenties, failure to keep pace with your peer group…these are the signs that parents must look at and look for.

8) A series of physical ailments which do not run a typical course and/or fail to respond to treatment. The doctor cannot help. Prayer is not helping. You keep getting sicker and sicker and sicker. Jesus called that an attack of the devil. Paul called it that, too. Why in the world must I call it a genetic defect?

9) Neglect of personal hygiene, disheveled, unsanitary surroundings. Exaggerated concern for order and for cleanliness. A full obsession – clean all through the night – or the extreme of it, as dirty as a pig with no concern and no regard, absolutely oblivious to their surroundings.

10) Difficulty adjusting to new people and places.

11) Undue anxiety and worry. Phobias. This is one I see all the time. Feelings of being persecuted.

12) Too much or too little sleep. This is another one that I see all the time. People whose lives have been reduced to this. Sleep becomes the only freedom they know, so they escape into sleep. Their form of recreation is to go to bed. They run to it. It is their company. It is their constant buddy. It is the way they escape from questions, from probing, from harassment, from human contact. They go to sleep, almost like a trance, almost like walking around with an IV with morphine in it. They have trained themselves to the point that their body produces the kinds of endorphins that give them a state of euphoria and they fall asleep at the drop of a hat. You would be amazed at the amount of people who are like that. They think, "If I have ten, fifteen, or twenty minutes, I can catch a nap." Regardless of whether the world is falling apart, they will hide in sleep.

13) Excessive self-centeredness, indifference to other people's feelings, doings, ideas. Lack of sympathy with other people's pains or needs.

14) Substantial rapid weight loss or gain.

15) Muted, flat emotions. Absence of anger, delight, or sorrow. Reactions to stimuli or inappropriate emotions. Sometimes sharp, inexplicable mood swings, silliness at serious moments, unpredictable tears. For older people, doctors are quick to tell you it is the menopausal/hormonal thing. Irrational behavior. Erratic behavior. Behavior almost equivalent to a Jekyll and Hyde.

2. I experienced that a few years ago in 1988. It was so severe, I remember having to go to the doctor and they put me on a medicine called Prozac. Now, Prozac is not a drug and that is why I

took it. I was very, very against anti-depressants. I would absolutely rather just drop backwards dead than to take any drug. So the doctor counseled me fully on the effects of Prozac and said it was not a drug. He said it would take fourteen days to get into my system, because I was having a real bad time.

3. I went on this prescription and after a while as it entered into my system. I was stabilized. I did not get excited, nor did I get sad. You could tell me the best joke you wanted and there was no humor in me. At the same time, you could drop dead and let your head fall off and roll like a basketball and it would not phase me. I was just flatlining. No emotions. Watch out for people who do not have any emotions. It is the sign of a deeply troubled spirit.

16) Negative self-image and outlook. Inferiority complex. Feelings of worthlessness.

17) Frequent, random changes of plans. Inability to stick with a job, a school, a program, a living arrangement. Failure to keep appointments or abide by decisions.

18) Extreme aggressive, combativeness, hostility, violence, rage, or exaggerated docility. On the one hand a loose cannon and a tiger from out of the wilds of the jungle, and on the other hand, "walk all over me, buddy, I don't care…I'm doing it for the glory of God." Refusal to confront or avoidance of argument. God says to be angry. He says do no sin with it, but He says to be angry.

19) Risk taking. A compulsiveness without good, sound wisdom. Jumping into situations and crash landing, and then thinking it

was a bad deal. Getting out of it and turning right around, not having learned a thing from the past experience, and jumping into another risky situation, such as relationships. Business. Get-rich-quick-schemes. A compulsiveness to get involved because you are driven by a force that says, "This time I'll make it. This time I'll go to the top." What a delusion!

20) Lack of zest and enthusiasm. Listlessness. Sadness. Mood habitually down. Limited or missing sense of humor.

3

THE TRUINE MAN

How can a demon spirit indwell the same body at the same time as the Holy Spirit? The New Testament word for spirit is "pneuma." In contradistinction from the natural or soulish, the spirit is the part of a man which has the ability to grasp and perceive divine things. I Corinthians 2:14 is where you will find the supporting scripture for this statement. This is crucial to all that I am going to say.

The word for soul is "psyche." This word defines the self-life. We are trichotomous beings. We are mind, we are body, and we are spirit, but the spirit of man is alone in itself in terms of the whole union of this three-part holistic view of man. New Age philosophy and modern medicine has taken the edge off that trichotomy and they have instituted a new word, "holistics".

Holistic medicine is medicine to treat the mind, body, and spirit. Man does not have that ability. The spirit is a mechanism of the Godhead that is put in you. It is the Spirit of God that is holistic. It is God in

Heaven who is a holistic God because He is dealing with a trichotomous man, a man who is mind, body, and spirit.

I would not support the idea that your spirit could be possessed, but I would support the idea of your soul being possessed, because it is in the realm of the self-life. It is in the realm of the sensory knowledge life and it is the area of the being, the mind part of the being that is captivated by the illusion or illusions, and is controlled because of the thinking. Thought patterns of a man are now changed.

The scripture in Ephesians 2:1 teaches that prior to salvation, a man is dead in his trespasses and in his sins. Jesus comes into the human spirit and brings His life. The absolute and total delivering process is when Jesus comes into the mind of man.

Philippians 2:5 says,

"Let this mind be in you, which was also Christ Jesus:"

He comes into the spirit and He brings the spirit of His life into your spirit, and then when we are totally and completely transformed through the process of deliverance, the mind of Christ occupies our soulish realm.

The word for salvation found in Philippians 2:13-15 is interpreted "soteria." Thayer's Lexicon gives the primary meaning of this word as "deliverance from the molestation of enemies." Soteria…salvation. It is the rescue from the trouble of adversaries. The picture becomes clear. Jesus has delivered our spirit from the power of Satan. Now He says to us, "Work out your own deliverance from the molestation of enemies until you have freed both soul and body." So how can anyone, in the face of such a good word, still hold to a position that is absolutely unfounded – that a Christian cannot have a demon?

If anybody asks me if a Christian can have a demon, I simply say, "He can have anything he wants to," and I drop the issue. He can have a drink. He can have an extra wife. My goodness, why couldn't he have a demon? He can have anything he wants.

DECEPTION FOLLOWS FALSE TEACHING

The result when we deny that demonization of Christians is possible and that this cannot happen to us is that false teaching would be perpetuated. An erroneous and unscriptural position that believers cannot have a demon is false teaching.

These results follow:

1) The old sin nature becomes the whipping boy and the middle ground between God and demons. If we deny we can have a demon, we go on practicing the way we have practiced, and our old sin nature beats the living daylights out of us and constantly robs us where we can never be on top. We never have anything. We are always robbed. We are always poverty-stricken. We are always losing because we have failed to acknowledge a very basic truth…a spirit is giving us hell!

2) All problems are thought to be due to the lack surrender, and we yield all we know to sacrifice, and we are still getting flogged morning, noon, and night. To just surrender is erroneous. It is beyond relinquishment. Surrender itself, is good…we have a need to yield to enter first into the initial place where

God's spirit sanctifies and makes us whole. We have to submit for that.

3) People are left open to be snared into cults by "angels of light." They deny this stuff, and they are going to get themselves a king-sized demon who comes as an angel of light and takes them off to Waco and finally burns them in a house. Don't believe in it? Just submit yourself to it and that is what can happen to you if you don't believe.

4) All inherited characteristics are thought to be unchangeable. "My Grandfather was like that." "My uncle on my mother's side third removed from me – he was like that." "My Aunt Jean is like that and somehow I picked it up and I'm like that." Inherited characteristics seem to be thought of as unchangeable.

5) Personality quirks and characteristics are thought to be unchangeable.

6) It makes us unable to break the bondage of another person's will. If you say, "That's just the way he is. Forget praying about change because that is the way he is." Then you do not pray about change. You do not want to invade or prevail over his will, so that the boy would stop being a devil out of hell. Do not prevail over him. That is the way he is. His grandfather passed that on to him. That is lie out of the pit of hell!

7) Mental health programs which teach all problems are the result of heredity are supported.

8) Demons are given legal ground to stay when a person sits under the teaching that denies a Christian can have a demon.

9) Demonic lies about oppression, possession, etc., are perpetuated.

10) It reinforces spiritual pride which keeps leaders from re-examining their teachings and retracting error. There is coming a time, and the time is now, when we must re-evaluate our teachings and our preaching in the light of the Word of God. Get with the program. Study the Word of God. Ask for rhema word for revelatory experience. Get new and fresh anointing for the study of the Word of God, because there is not going to be a whole section in heaven with ignorant people. When I make it to heaven, I will not scrape in there on my belly, barely getting in and climbing over the fence. I will walk triumphantly into the gates of Heaven!

11) Despair and hopelessness are fostered within the demonized. Despair and hopelessness become your meat. They become the thing you feed on. It becomes your countenance. It becomes your life. It becomes all of you. You are one big, moving, despairing, hopeless junky.

12) It gives ground to accept as law all medical diagnoses and medication, and in the same tone, we jump up singing "Whose report will you believe? I will believe the report of the Lord!"

The following statistic I quote from an article called "The Children's Hour", U.S. News and World Report. The article was entitled "In One Day" We are now a few years beyond that, so as you are fully aware, we have come nearly thirty years since I read that article.

The article stated that 2,753 teenagers get pregnant; 1,099 teenagers have abortions; 367 teens miscarry; 1,287 teenagers give birth; 666 babies are born to women who have had inadequate prenatal care; 72 babies die before one month of life; 110 babies die before their first birthday; nine children die from gunshot wounds; five teenagers commit suicide; 609 teenagers get Gonorrhea or Syphilis; 988 children are abused; 3,288 children run away from home; 49,322 children are in public juvenile correctional facilities; 2,269 illegitimate children are born; and 2,989 kids see their parents divorced, of whom a large number are Christians; all in one day.

I would assume that we have almost quadrupled that statistic currently. You tell me that we do not have demons. You tell me these kids that see divorce have not come from Christian homes or Christian parents splitting up. You tell me these kids with these pregnancies and maladies have not been raised in good, godly homes. You tell me that there is not a demonic influence against our cities and our churches and our nation. You tell me that? I dare to say, you are wrong sir or ma'am. It is experience that will become the cutting edge for you and I, instead of ignorance. It is demons, spiritual wickedness in high places, principalities and powers, rulers of darkness, assignments on the family, on the home, on the church, and on the school.

PRESSURE MAKES PERFECT

In the Greek, "believer" indicates one relying on Jesus Christ for salvation. In Acts 5:14, the word means unadulterated trust. In I Timothy 4:12, trueness to entrust one's spiritual faith, assurance, well-being. A check list for believers is this, therefore: They must bear fruit. – John 15:2. Signs shall follow them. – Mark 16:17, 18. They shall do works

Jesus did. – John 14:12. Answered prayer. – John 15:7. A friend of Jesus. – John 15:14. Witnessing. – John 15:27.

What about demons in Christians? Listen to Paul. He says,

"When you are assembled in the name of our Lord Jesus and I am with you in spirit, and the power of our Lord Jesus is present, hand this man over to Satan, so that the sinful nature may be destroyed and his spirit saved on the day of the Lord."

I Corinthians 5:4-5

Sounds like Paul understands possession, and he says if you do not act right, you are going to get whipped into shape.

My mother always said as I was growing up, "Hard ears- you won't hear. Own way – you're going to feel." I did not take time to even try to understand that. I was too young. Still, every time she reprimanded me, the stick would come down. "Hard ears – you won't hear. Own way – you're going to feel." Over a period of several years, I finally got it. When you do not hear and when you do not attend, you are going to feel the pain of correction.

I think Christians are representative of a kettle. Those old kettles that you put water in and it has a little whistle at the top. You turn up the fire, and when the water is boiled and ready, it begins to whistle. This is the ideal position for a Christian. Water up to the throat, fire in the behind, and your whistling – whew!

That is the ideal concept of a Christian. Under fire… choking with the cares of the world, but boy, you are sending off a signal saying, "I'm ready. Use me!"

RE - THINKING PERSONAL BIBLICAL INTERPRETATION

Scripture after scripture shows a principle. If you sleep on the job, the enemy is going to creep in on you. It is no secret many have become discouraged and filled with awful despair.

Ernest B. Roxted has a tract called "Demon Activity in the Christian." In it he says,

"Experience of course is not the basis for the interpretation of the Bible. Nevertheless, if consistent experience runs counter to an interpretation, the dedicated seeker after truth will set out to find the reason. He must be willing to restudy his interpretation under the direction of the Holy Spirit and be prepared to make any necessary corrections in his own beliefs so as to be in full agreement with the facts as they are." He further points out, "Understanding the Biblical doctrine of human depravity should cause one to wonder if the Holy Spirit would enter a person under any circumstances."

There is an excellent presentation of the whole question in the book "Can a Christian have a Demon?" by Don Basham. Non-charismatic writers like Francis Manuel, Merle Unger, Mark Bubeck, and Robert Peterson also teach that a Christian can have a demon.

In his very balanced and scholarly treaties, Dr. Unger writes,

"In demon influence, evil spirits exhort power over a person short of actual possession. Such influence may vary from mild harassment to extreme subjection when body and mind became dominated and held in slavery by spirit agents."

A member of the church in Corinth seems to have been overcome by a spirit of lust.- I Corinthians 5:1-5. Jesus rebuked a spirit of fever in Peter's mother-in-law in Luke 4:38 and 39, and he left her and she was well. In Mark 3:33 and Mark 9:25, Jesus uses the same term to rebuke Satan. Sickness is describes as an oppression of the devil in Acts 10:38. Jesus often healed by removing spirits of infirmity which are simply another method of satanic attack. Consider Peter, one moment he spoke of divine revelation declaring that Jesus is the very Christ, the Rock, and the next moment, he was reprimanded by Jesus, who said to him,

"Thou savorest not the things that be of God,"
and rebuked Satan in him.

Luke 5:1-11 is paraphrased. These guys were fishing all night long and they had caught nothing. Jesus came on the scene and He encouraged them to launch out into the deep. Based on the knowledge of sensory perception, they said, "We've been fishing all night and we've caught nothing. How dare you, are you going to change the elements?" Jesus said to them, "I tell you. Go out there into the deep. Go out there into uncharted waters. Go out there where it is unfamiliar territory. There are treasures out there to be discovered." They replied to Him, "Nevertheless, at Your word, I will do it." What a catch! We are launching out into the deep. It is unfamiliar, uncharted territory for many, but there are treasures out there beyond your wildest imagination.

4

CONFRONTATION OF A HOLY GOD

When you engage the enemy in warfare, do not think for a moment. He is going to lie down and play dead. If you think that, you will have a black eye, a busted nose, and a broken head coming. You will be battered and bruised if you think the enemy is going to lie down and die because you challenged him. Be ready for a fight, because we are talking warfare. We are not going out there into battle until we understand that God sees us in a particular way and God expects from us, a particular behavior. When we have that figured out, we can walk triumphantly into battle because,

"Greater is He that is in you than he that is in the world."

Isaiah 6:1-8 says,

"In the year that King Uzziah died, I saw the Lord Seated on a throne, high and exalted, and the train of His robe filled the temple. Above Him were seraphs, each with six wings: With two

wings they covered their faces, with two they covered their feet, and with two they were flying. And they were calling to one another: 'Holy, holy, holy is the Lord almighty; the whole earth is full of His glory.' At the sound of their voices the door posts and thresholds shook and the temple was filled with smoke. 'Woe to me!' I cried. 'I am ruined! For I am a man of unclean lips, and I live among a people of unclean lips, and my eyes have seen the King, the Lord Almighty.' Then one of the seraphs flew to me with a live coal in his hand, which he had taken with tongs from the alter. With it, he touched my mouth and said, 'See, this has touched your lips; Your guilt is taken away and your sin atoned for.' Then I heard the voice of the Lord saying, 'Whom shall I send?

And who will go for Us?' And I said, 'Here am I.

Send me!' "

A response to holiness. Isaiah lived all of his life in the shadow of Uzziah. So much so that he could not see God. It took death, the ultimate separation, for Isaiah to finally look up and see God in His holiness.

Did you ever walk into a room and you are not really dressed "cool," but everybody else in the room is dressed "cool?" Something about that makes you feel like you do not belong there, doesn't it? Has that happened to you before? Somebody invited you out, but they did not tell you how to dress, so you showed up in jeans, tennis shoes, and an old T-shirt. Then you step in and everyone is in three-piece suits. There is a sudden sense of how out of place you are.

Spiritually, Isaiah saw God, and the awesomeness of God caused Isaiah to look within himself and he thought, "I am a man of unclean lips.

Woe is me! I am really, really dirty." Confrontation of a Holy God always produces a holy response in us. "God, I am dirty before you!"

A while back I knew that I was not living right, but at the same time I was pastoring. This is a tremendous admission. I was preaching to a couple of hundred people every weekend, running a big church, and not living right. The Spirit of God brought such conviction and such chastisement upon me that I had to lock myself away for seven days.

For seven days I did not see the outside. I took a black garbage bag and sealed my window. I didn't even let the light come through. I was desperate. I was so unclean before God, I did not even want light to shine on me. I saw the Holiness of God through His work. I saw His expectations of me. I saw from God's viewpoint where I should be and as I confronted where I should be, I realized that I was so far away, I was not even in the same city that God was in dwelling totally removed from an active experience with God or Godly living. I am about to the point of a process that would culminate in, "Here I am Lord, send me."

What was interesting, to paraphrase, those were my last words at the end of the seven days when the oppression broke in my spirit. I was flat on my back, weak as a dog, and I simply lay down and said, "God, I will do whatever You want me to do. I will go wherever You want me to go. I will say whatever You want me to say."

Since then, to the best of my ability, I have been going, doing, and saying what God instructs me to do. Oh, it has caused me problems many times. Confrontation with a Holy God will always produce holiness on the part of the believer. "Here am I, God, send me." When you walk into the presence of God, something revolutionary and radically changes within your being. Isaiah could not see God for anything. The

King was his idol. What are our idols? I could not begin to imagine. I am sure money is somewhere on the list. When it becomes an obsession, it becomes a really big idol. It could be your kids, your wife, your possessions, your house, your car- a multitude of different things. Sometimes these things must be removed in order for us to see God.

King Uzziah died and then Isaiah sees the Lord high and lifted up and there is a real confrontation with himself. For the first time, he stands and as he stands in the presence of God, he sees how unclean he is. Many, many, many a dysfunction will never be alleviated until we stand in the presence of God. Many difficult relations, many difficult problems, many maladies of all sorts and proportions will never begin to even break or lift until we step into the presence of the Holy God. Until we do, we have nothing to compare our life to or with. When we stand in the presence of God, we see our uncleanness and where our heart is. If we never entered that arena, where would our conviction be, what would we measurement for mankind. When we stand in God's presence like Isaiah did, we realize we are unclean. When we really want to break through, step into the holiness of God through His Word and see how unclean a being we might be.

A LESSON FROM PETER

Look at Peter's example. There are a few things we might learn looking at Peter's life. One is surrender. The second is his obedience. The third is his faith. The fourth is his insight. Matthew 4:18-19, is the combination of the scripture that talks about making them fishers of men. Jesus comes by and says, "Follow me and I'll make you fishers of men." Peter dropped his net and headed off with Jesus. Absolute surrender. It is not questioned. We do not question God. If only we were disciplined to respond when Jesus comes by and says to come follow Him, we would say, "That's it. That's all I need to hear." What a tremendous release it would be not to have to debate the issue. God has requirements for us. We say "But where am I going to hear God?"

We hear God through His Word. Just surrender to His Word. Just lay down the fight, lay down the resistance, lay down the rebellion, and follow God's Word. It still gives direction. It is still His map. It is still the GPS for our lives. We cannot go wrong following it. We will not be deceived.

I heard about a well-known preacher whose church was picketed. He preached some wrong doctrine, so they picketed his church. We cannot be deceived if we read the Word for ourselves. Will you believe everything you are told?

My good friend is a police officer. He went into the confessional and was confessing his sins to the priest. At the same time he was talking to the priest, a truck was dropping some gravel off in the church yard and they were putting it down in the wrong place. The priest left the confessional, went outside, and cursed the driver out. Here is my friend repenting of his sins to the priest in the confessional booth, and he hears the priest cursing a man outside in the yard. That was not the problem. The problem is that he went to a man to tell him of his sins, a human instrument.

Here is the problem with that. The priest is a human and is subject to error, so the absolving of his sin was contingent upon the priest being able to tell God exactly what you told him. Suppose you had a whole lot of sins. You might be in trouble because the priest would forget some of that and if he did not tell it to God, you are still holding that with you. Then you are in big trouble!

Read the Word. Do not depend on a man to bring salvation to you or absolve you or get you free. The answer is in the Word. Get the Word for yourself because man is subject to error. Do not look at preachers who are reporting the truth, and I am not saying they are erroneous people, but we are not your answer. Jesus is the answer. We are street signs. We point the way in which to go, but we are not the way to go. That is the tragedy of people vesting all their interest in a man who says he has the ultimate cure. We say, " I want him to lay hands on me because he has power and the demons are going to leave and the maladies will be corrected." If we live right, we will not even need them.

Peter surrendered. He was obedient. Luke 5:4-10 says they were fishing all night and did not catch anything. Jesus came and told them to cast their nets out. I can see Peter, "It's full moon. That's when we fish. It's high tide. That's when we fish. I have been out here all night long and I haven't caught a single fish. You are telling me to go back out there and throw my net again. Let me tell you something. Fishing I know. Feeding hungry people you know. Mind your own business." I can see how Peter's attitude would be like that.

Instead he says, not necessarily in a disgruntled tone, but my evangelistic mind wants to make it look like a disgruntled tone, "Okay, because you say so, I guess I'll do it. Nevertheless at Your word, you say to throw it back out in the deep and I'll go." Jesus tells Peter to go and fish in the same place he had been fishing before. "Now that you've done it your way and you didn't catch any fish, do it my way and see if you will catch a fish."

How many of us really think we know ourselves? "I know me and I dare to argue because a man with an experience has it all. I know me. Do not try to tell me about me. I know me." Does that not sound like the basis of a lot of arguments between people? "You know what I'm thinking, huh? You're inside my head and you know what's going on inside of me? I know me better than you. Who died and made you God? I know me." We do not know anything!

Paul says, "I do not want to know anything except Jesus Christ and Him crucified." Understanding ourselves and knowing who we are is a kind of arrogance because it defeats us in terms of victory. We are going to hold on to who we are until death do us part. In terms of helping dysfunction and resolving conflicts, one of the first things we need to start with is to forget what we think we know and start from scratch. I do not know anything. God, come and teach me everything I need to know. All we have known so far has not helped us, so really we do not know a whole lot. We do not know anything except God's wisdom comes and imparts it to us because all that we know has not brought us out of problems. We are still in problems so start from zero. "God, I do not know. Teach me."

Faith. Peter sees an apparition coming on the water. To make a long story short, he finally realizes it is Jesus. He says, "Master, if you would bid me to come, I will come." So Jesus tells him, "come." If you just tell me to come, I will. If God could instruct you how to change, would you be willing to change. If God would impart deep truths to the heart to break the bondage, would you be willing to step out on the water with God? Peter stepped out into the water and fixed his gaze upon Jesus. Now let's go back to the beginning.

It took faith to step out of the boat. It took faith to break all conventional wisdom. You do not walk on water. When God gives you a faith word for restoring, relieving, and rebuilding, you have to step out in place. You are journeying into a place where you know the hands that are there to receive you, are safe hands. You are safe in the hands of God. In the process of reconstruction, you have to take a bold faith move and do something that is unconventional. You walk on water, metaphorically speaking.

Mark 8:27-30 says,

"And Jesus went on with his disciples to the villages of Caesarea Philippi; and on the way He asked His disciples, 'Who do people say that I am?' And they answered Him, 'John the Baptist; and others say, Elijah; but others, one of the prophets.' And He asked them, 'But who do you yourselves say that I am?' Peter replied to Him, 'You are the Christ, the Messiah, the Anointed One.' And He charged them sharply to tell no one about Him."

Surrender, obedience, faith, and insight. When it gets through to us that He is the Christ, the Anointed One, it is the beginning of wisdom because the fear of the Lord is the beginning of wisdom. When we understand that, discernment has just begun to knock on our door. The answer to our problem is simply this, He is the Christ. He is the Anointed One. He is the Messiah. Discern that. This is the mystery unlocked.

5

WALKING IN THE SPIRIT, NOT IN THE FLESH

I chronicles 16:9- "the eyes of the Lord run to and fro above the earth on behalf of those whose hearts are fixed toward Him. But you have done a foolish thing." This scripture is the kind of thing that is repulsive at the very beginning. Can the Word of God be repulsive? It is the kind of thing that is a little bit hard to take at the very beginning, but I tell you there is such discipline in that scripture that you learn to almost chastise yourself in that Word. "God's eyes are upon those whose hearts are fixed toward him," but when we do a foolish thing, we will be at war. There will be no rest for us; we will be at war. God wants to move upon this people. I can almost feel the heart of the Father (not that I am closer to Him that anyone else), but there is such an eagerness in Christ that God wants to impart to this people for this particular time more so than ever.

BUILDING A FOUNDATION IN THE SPIRIT

The Word of God is like a two-edged sword. It separates. The Word of God surgically removes in excellence minute errors and divides truth from error. A careful study of the Word of God will set us on the right path.

Hebrews 4:12-13 says,

For the Word of God is quick, and powerful, and sharper than any two-edged sword, piercing even to the dividing asunder of soul and spirit, and of the joints and marrow, and it is a discerner of the thoughts and intents of the heart. Neither is there any creature that is not manifest in His sight: but all things are naked and opened unto the eyes of Him with whom we have to do."

Nothing is hidden that will not be revealed. No darkness, no deceit, no diabolical treachery, no forms of compromise. There is nothing hidden that will not be revealed. There is no element of the Word of God that will remain a mystery. There may be a mystery in the application and manifestation of the Word such as marriage, the one flesh concept is a mystery. I still do not understand why through the act of submitting to God or to your wife can produce a healthy body.

This is a mystery, but there is no mystery in the Word about that concept. The chemistry of how this is performed will always be a mystery to my mind, but there is no mystery in its explanation in the Word of God.

There is no mystery in terms of the promises of God for us. However, involved in the promises of God to us are conditions which are also not mysterious. So there is no need to say or confess, "This is a hard thing and I cannot fulfill it."

Whenever I preach on heart purity, I divide people. I do not like dividing people and they are not divided along theological lines. They are divided along the lines of compromise and commitment. How much am I willing to give so I may receive all of God that I am able to take? How much am I willing to be yielded up so I might receive the fullness of the measure of Christ in me? It divides. People just do not want to live that way. "You ask a hard thing. You mean I have to give up my pleasures? You mean I have to abandon myself and the things that I like and enjoy? You mean I have to live a dull, boring life? It cuts across the lines of pleasure.

Philosophically speaking, one of the modern-day philosophers, I think it was Immanuel Kant who said this in his philosophy statement,

"Man is a pleasure-seeking, pain-avoiding creature."

What sound doctrine for sinners! Isn't that the truth? I seek pleasure. I avoid pain. It produces the path of least resistance. That only sounds good, but it is a cop-out. The path of least resistance is a cop-out. It shows no sense of accountability. If we want to ride high on the hog, we are going to pay the price for that ride. Accountability must come if we want to be a pleasure-seeking, pain-avoiding creature, but we do not touch that aspect of the philosophy.

THE GLORY OF GOD

God promises to us a covering. Exodus 33:22 reads,

"When My glory passes by, I will put you in a cleft in the rock and cover you with My hand until I have passed by."

Moses could not withstand the presence and the glory of God. It was an awesome thing. It was a powerful thing. The glory of God. I have not come to terms with the fullness of the scope of that as yet, the glory of God. We have this thing we throw out – the glory of God – the manifested presence of God come down to dwell within and around us. It sounds so highly theological and so Godly that I am even excited to say "the glory of God."

The glory of God is the goodness of God. Now that is simple is it not? God's healing is His glory. God's provision is His glory. God making a way when there is no way, is His glory. Every good and perfect gift that comes from the Father above is His glory. The glory of God is the goodness of God, and however that goodness manifests itself to us individually as per our need, that is the glory of God.

God promises to us that "I will cover you in the cleft of the rock because you cannot contain My glory when it passes by." It is so much, it is so big that this mortal being will disintegrate in the presence of the ultimate glory of God. He had to hide Moses in a rock because he could not withstand the glory of God. He said, "You cannot look at this thing. I'll let you feel it when it passes by, but you cannot look at this thing." It is so big. It is so good. It is beyond our mind to perceive. Our head would explode with the glory of God and yet He promises, "I will cover you with that glory." The glory of God is His deliverance.

He says,

"This uncontainable glory that I have for you, this expression of the ultimate of the Godhead that you cannot contain, this is yours. I will hide you in the cleft of the rock and you will behold with your eyes, not the immediate glory, but you will behold the effects of my glory as it passes by."

I am going to see vile, corrupt beings turn to call God blessed. I am going to see people who were heathens rise up to sing "Jesus is Lord." The glory of God is passing by and we will see the effects of it, for we cannot contain the glory of God to look in His face, for no man has seen the face of God and live, but we have seen the glory of God. He says this is His promise, but this promise has with it a condition and every promise that God gives has a condition.

When I was small and growing up, we had a statement in Trinidad. We said, "Nothing for nothing and very little for a penny." If we want to put out a penny's worth of our sacrifice to God, very little for a penny. If we put none out for God, nothing is coming back. This life is going to cost us. Do we want to walk in deliverance? It is going to cost us something. At the very outset, it is going to cost our heart, purity. He says, "I will cover you, but here is the condition for my covering: You must be submitted to me."

UNDERSTANDING REAL SUBMISSION

Do you understand submission? Are you willing to listen to your wife? Are you having trouble with the condition? Are you willing to listen to the weaker vessel impart to you knowledge and wisdom and truth and guidance according to the Holy Spirit? I am not talking manipulation, domination, intimidation, and control. I am talking about a relationship whereby you respect your wife.

Part of the problem with the church is that we have too many marriages that are off-balanced. We have too many one-sided, power trip, egomaniac marriages. We have a bunch of "macho" men who think they know it all and will not listen to their wives, and half of the time I tell you, they are looking out for your own best interest. Trying to protect you from being stupid and doing stupid things, and you cannot listen long enough to take good, godly advice, and you end up in mess over and over again. If you want deliverance, you will go home and before you can say a word after you get in the door, you get on your knees begging your wife to forgive you for being stupid for so long, and begging that she will forgive you for being egotistical, big-headed, and downright stupid, That is deliverance. That is the powerful ministry deliverance.

On the other hand, women need to understand that they are the weaker sex; understand that you compliment a relationship. You do not subdue it, you compliment it. You compliment a relationship with your husband. Once you get into marriage, you must understand the concept of interdependency. Interdependency is the concept of, "I need you, but sure as I stand here, you need me." Interdependency is a concept of marriage that is so archaic, obsolete, antiquated, it is a seemingly foreign concept to marriages.

Women, you can do more to hurt a man, and more so, a man in the ministry. The devil takes aim at you. He uses you oftentimes as a whipping boy against your husband. You get so risen up with pride. You get so caught up in the things that are not really important, and you miss the big picture that you are to compliment and be a helpmate to your husband. You are not to run him ragged. You are not to have him like a little boy on a leash pulling him about at your whim and fancy. You have to understand godly authority and godly placing. You are helpmate to compliment in the marriage, not to subdue it.

We have so many "Jezebel's" on the loose. Remember Jezebel? She was a woman who when she did not get her husband's approval, she drafted her own plan anyway. When we set up this ungodly system in our homes, the sanctuary of our beings goes out of order, and then we come to the corporate body, we bring so many dysfunctional churches into the corporate body that we cannot see our head from our feet. We cannot see clear, we are so messed up. We are in a daze. We are in a fog. We cannot be true. People need deliverance. We need to counsel for hours on end and the simple truth is, get your house in order! Learn to submit to your husband. Learn to submit to the godly care that has been put over you It is no wonder why the ministry is in such a mess. We do not respect pastors anymore. We do not care about them. We could not care less if they sit or spin.

Let me take you into a little Jewish history for a moment. To a Jewish man growing up from which we take the concept of our modern-day Christianity, I document, and this is not hearsay…this is intensive research: a rabbi, a Jewish custom that should a man and his rabbi be held ransom, a man's first obligation is to free his spiritual covering before he frees his physical covering because the spiritual covering oversees the spirit of his life. It is more important eternally for us to be concerned about our spiritual covering than our biological: We have lost respect for our coverings. It would only be fair to say that sometimes in the past and even in the present, men of God have been ruthless in their pursuits and have dishonored God and broke the trust that man has put in them. They will be accountable unto God.

GOD'S PROMISES OF FORGIVENESS

He promises forgiveness. Psalms 78:38-39 reads,

"Yet He was merciful; He forgave their iniquities and did not destroy them. Time after time He restrained His anger and did not stir up His full wrath. He remembered that they were but flesh, a passing breeze that does not return."

I spoke with a man who is angry at God. From my experience with him, I have known him to be a godly man. As far as my sensory knowledge and spiritual discernment goes, I had the highest regard for this man. He is very sick and he cannot understand his sickness, and lately he has told me that he is of the firm belief that God is a homosexual. This a God-fearing man who because of affliction has turned his anger toward God. God says that He is willing to extend mercy, considering that this man is only as a breath or as a piece of grass that can wither away. God is forgiving. God is willing to extend mercy to people who have gone to such a place, who have been so abused by the devil that they are beginning to blame God for it.

God is still willing to extend forgiveness to such a person. That forgiveness will come only through repentance. Repentance is first godly sorrow, and it is also turning around. We must be sorry for our sins. We have got to be able, with passion and resolve in us, to say, "God, I am sorry…not because I got caught." Repentance when we get caught just does not sit well with me. Repentance is godly sorrow, but beyond godly sorrow, it is turning around. It is, "I used to go this way…I will now go this way." It is turning around when we come to a place where our sensory knowledge in the Spirit witness to us that we should apologize and say, "God, have mercy. Be merciful unto me." At that point in time, be prepared to turn completely around and go with God in a new godly direction.

CULT TRAPPING

He promises anointing. I John 2:27 says,

> *"But as for you, the anointing, the sacred appointment, the unction, which you received from Him abides permanently in you; so then you have no need that anyone should instruct you. But just as His anointing teaches you concerning everything and is true and is no falsehood, so you must abide, live in, never to depart from Him, being rooted in Him, knit to Him, just as His anointing has taught you to do."*

That particular verse is quoted from the Amplified Bible because it says so much. It says an anointing abides in you. It lives in you. So often we misconstrue this scripture to say, "The anointing abides in me so I do not need anybody to teach me." That is not what it is saying. It is saying, as Jesus' anointing, and unction continues to exist as the ongoing, working relationship of the believer and the Father we are taught by that anointing. It does not preclude or exclude any other outside form of training we may receive. But as far as spiritual revelatory discernment in the things of God, the deep things of God, the rhema things of God that abide in the Spirit in us, this teaches us, and we have no need to go find an outside source to complement that form of learning.

Example in point are those people who are of a particular persuasion who believe the Word of God, but there is another book that must go along with it because to them, the Bible alone is not sufficient. Here is the Bible, but here is this book. The Bible is incomplete without this book with which our dear brother saint so and so, received a revelatory experience from God while on a camel's back in the desert of Saudi Arabia, and so he has put in print these deep truths that were missing in the Word, and in order to understand that, you must have this to go along with it. We have one word for that in the Christian faith and it is called "cult." There is an easy way to define a cult – a simple mathematical formula: First it adds to the Word. Secondly it subtracts from the deity of Christ. Thirdly, it multiplies the need of works for salvation. And fourthly, it divides loyalty among the believers. Come our way. You do not have the truth; we have the truth. Addition, subtraction, multiplication, and division – watch out, for it is as subtle as a snake!

The anointing abides, and I do not need addition, subtraction, multiplication, and division. The anointing abides and I am taught by the Spirit, in the Spirit, the things of the Spirit that are pertinent for my walk. The anointing God provides has a condition – obedience.

He promises dominion. This dominion has a condition called accountability. He promise righteousness. But for the righteousness of God, there is a condition; the condition of judgement. Refrain from judging people. When we call somebody "fat," we are not really imparting any brand new divine revelation. Usually it is said with a certain amount of derogatory tone in it. "Look at that at person." Disgust comes out. This is a judgement that says not only are you fat, it says "stay fat." When we pass those kinds of judgement on people, we are not talking about a condition, we are talking about a statement that says, "I want you to stay that way."

We are actually releasing demonic forces to ensure they cannot break the chains and shackles that has gotten them in that place. We are releasing enough negative influence upon them to keep them like that, and they have been trying all they know how: starving themselves to death; running themselves ragged; not even sleeping, doing everything they know, and they cannot fight it because you and your snide, thin, model-sized figure look upon them in judgement and say, "Wow, what a big, fat pig goes there." People do that so callously. "He is so ugly." "He is so stupid."

Whenever I go to New York, in certain segments of the community that I visit the communal password in this New York neighborhood is, "What's up stupid?" This is how they greet people it's another form of greeting like ''How u doin''It is a curse from which we must purge our tongue. These little flippant things we talk about, we say them so casually without even thinking about it. We are pronouncing curses on people over and over and over.

TRUTH BRINGS DELIVERANCE

You want deliverance? These are the basic things. You expected me to jump on your head and seize some foreign little ugly monster standing on your head and rip its throat apart and stomp it on the ground? Is that what you expected. You expect me to lie to you and see some green, purple, and orange, ugly, hideous creature hanging around your shoulder and come across and slap it silly until it falls off your back, and then you think you are free? You are not free until there is truth in the inward parts.

We are in bondage when we are living a lie. You are in bondage when you cannot be honest with your wife. You are in bondage when you cannot be honest with your husband. Men lie to their wives because they think she is going to get mad at the truth. We lie because we believe the truth is going to get us in trouble. We must not live a lie because as long as we live in the remains of a lie, we are in bondage.

When you lie to your friends and you lie to your spouse and you lie to people in general, it becomes such a habit that you have developed the spirit of a pathological liar and you do not even know the truth. You are lying and you have deceived yourself and you think you are telling the truth because you have advanced into the state of a pathological liar and you cannot even discern when you are telling lies. Telling lies becomes a routine form of your daily existence, and you go through lying from one incident to another. Someone says, "How are you doing?" and maybe at that time you need twenty dollars, and you lie to them and say, "Man I sure have a need that is breaking my back. Oh God, hallelujah! My wife and I just barely made it up here." You know your tank's full of gas and you are lying to create sympathy so somebody will feel sorry for you. You are living in bondage and it does not matter or phase you in the least bit. You will go onto the next lie, then the next lie, and person after person all day long. You tell lies and half truths and you color it up. You exaggerate. You are a pathological liar and you are in bondage.

RE-TRAINING MAN

How do you train this man? How do you train this wild animal? Let me introduce a New Testament Greek word – praotes. This word is very applicable when we talk about the soul. Praotes is the ability to take an untamed, wild, ferocious, undomesticated being, and train him, culture him, control him, regulate his behavior to such a given extent that he now becomes encultured into a new environment and adapted to that environment even though foreign to himself and behave with harmony and exist peaceably in that new environment. In simple layman's terms: Go to India. Get yourself the wildest Bengal tiger. Bring it into the circus. Train it to act, jump through hoops, through fire, dance on a ball, roll on a stick, and behave like a human when instead when he would rather rip your throat apart and drink your blood. That is praotes. That is the meaning of praotes – to tame the wild. To make domesticated the wild, animalistic nature of a beast or man, or even better a demonical-influenced person; to bring them into harmony with their environment; to co-exist peacefully with other human beings that share this global atmosphere.

This is how you train your soul. That is how you bring the flesh under control. You do not tell some wild tiger to sit for the first time and then turn your back and think he is going to sit. You would be industrial strength stupid! It is a period of repetitive, Holy Ghost guidance, and patience working together in the Spirit of the Lord with the wisdom of God from on high that He gives without partiality and unbiased to the believer that brings you to the place of maturity.

A praotes believer is a mature believer. When you were a child, you acted like a child; you spoke like a child; you played like a child; you had temper tantrums like a child. But now that you have become a man, you will put away childish things; you will put away childish temper tantrums; you will put away childish clinging and longings for your toys. The only difference between men and boys is the price of their toys. We get so obsessed with our toys or acquisitions, and we need to put that under submission .

Do you remember pharaoh? He would rather have one more night with the frogs; he would rather have one more night with the flies than to let the people of God go. His idols had risen up so high that he could not release them. The funny thing about it is, everything that became an idol, God ruined it.

The River Nile was an idol to the Egyptians. They had the best water, the cleanest, the purest, and they could not see God. So the River Nile became an idol and God spoiled their idol by turning it into blood. They had this goddess called Hext whose symbol was a frog because of its ability to regenerate itself. It came from the mud and would regenerate itself. They began to worship its regeneration powers to the extent they could not see God, so God took the frog, the symbol of the goddess Hext, and gave them more frogs than they could bear. Frogs everywhere! God spoke to them to let His people go. No? One more night with the frogs.

They began to worship the ground because it brought forth such good fruit. We have plenty. We have abundance. We have the biggest, the nicest, the best, the juiciest, and they worshipped it, so God took the very sand in the garden place and turned it into lice. You think that was bad enough? He hit them by the water, He hit them by the goddess, He hit them by lice that He turned from the sand – earth, water, vegetation.

They began to worship the air that they had in Egypt. That became a god, The air that they breathed. God released a dose of flies on them, and still Pharaoh shouted, "One more night with the files," rather than submit and subdue.

We could go through all the plagues. God was coming against every idol they set up in their lives, and the same God of yesterday, today, and forever, will reduce every idol in our life. He will take it down. That is not punishment. Do not confuse it with punishment. "I am a jealous God and I will have no other gods before me." That is a law of Heaven. You cannot put up your toy? God is going to break it for you. I am not preaching that God is an abuser; He is good God. But if you start crowding the picture between you and God, He is going to clear the skies.

We need to train ourselves. We need to train our bodies. We need to train our kids. We need to train our families. Let's look at examples of training.

Proverbs 22:6

"Train a child in the way he should go, and when he is old he will not turn from it."

If you give him the right set of training, when he gets old, he will not deviate from it. He will go the way you have taught him.

Jean Paul Sarte is who we consider a modern-day philosopher. He and people like Immanuel Kant, modern-day philosophers, and by that I mean within the last hundred years. Jean Paul Sarte developed this philosophy called existentialism. Simply put, existentialism says that you are a product of your environment. In other words, if I take you and put you in the jungle, and all you ever had contact with was wild animals and you had no ability to develop speech or social skills, you would grow up like a wild animal. Existentialism says you are a product of your environment. You are cultured, nurtured, and shaped by what is around you and you will reproduce that environment.

If all your church has in it is confusion, you would reproduce confusion. If all your church has is spiritual sleepiness, you would reproduce a sleepy bunch of people. You are your environment. If by culpability, by reasons of association with the body that you have come to assimilate into, you will in turn be a product of and will walk out a perfect replica of what prevails in that body. Train up a child in the way he should go, and when he is old enough, he will not depart from it. If you are preached the Word, you will go out a Word people.

We always take that scripture to wack our kids over the head. Train up a child in the way he should go and when he is old enough, he will not depart from it. Wack, wack. Train up a body of believers in the Word they should go, and as they grow older in the Word, they will not depart from it. The motivation behind this training should always be one of love and protection. Always.

Another Greek word – harmatia – it is a sin-concept word, but it is one of the most unique words because it is ambivalent in that it starts out from sin, but ends with love. Harmatia is the "sin" word as we have come to know in the English language. It simply means to miss the mark. There is a good side to that. The fact that you missed the mark means you are at least aiming for it.

A little while ago, I shot at a particular animal and missed it, but because of the power of the gun that I was using, concussion killed the animal. It floated up dead without a bruise on it. I was aiming for it, but I missed it. Because of the close proximity to my target, it was killed all the same. Harmatia is to miss the mark that you were aiming for, and that mark should be the mark of excellence.

Now let me explain how you missed the mark. Any time you fire a weapon, there are elements to consider why you miss. One is recoil. I have to compensate – go under the target so that with recoil when it comes up, I hit my mark. I have to compensate for another factor called trajectory. After a bullet travels so long and collision with the molecular structure of the atmosphere, it begins to descend. I also have to compensate for wind. These are basic factors.

Here is the factor within harmatia that will make you miss. If as you aim at the target and you do not have love in your heart, you will miss the mark. Love is the perfect trajectory. If you cannot love and move from a motivation of love, you will miss the target every time. That is how harmatia begins as sin and ends up as a lack of pure love. To summarize this whole thing, if you cannot love purely, you will sin.

6

THE SOUL MAN

There are some different types of souls we deal with. Remember, the soul is that aspect of the being that controls will, intellect, and emotion. There is a kind of trichotomy to the soul. We are trichotomous beings. But within the realm of the soul, we have three facets of the soul: the will, the intellect, and emotion, and let me add deceit of your consciousness. This is where you get conscious from, both conscious and subconscious – from the pit of your subconscious being which becomes a trap or receptacle for all your physical manifestations.

The difference in great men and men that are not so great is, great men dream dreams and pursue them. Weak men with a slumbering spirit do not dream. They stumble from day to day. They do not dream anything. The subconscious mind does not know truth from error. That is why when you dream, you dream you are married to the most beautiful woman, you live in the biggest house, you have four Lexus's, and even your dog has a Cadillac Escalade. You dream fantastic dreams and as far as that goes there is no sense of unreality. You wake up and you are so defeated because your subconscious, which is a part of the soul that we do not address does not know fantasy from reality.

When the Spirit possesses all of your being, even your dreams will take on a god-like atmosphere. You will be in the middle of the night dreaming some kind of nonsense and some mechanism turns on from the depth of your dream and switches it off and tells you it is not real.

From the depth of your soul there is will, emotion, intellect, deceit of your consciousness, and the subconscious mind. That is why it is so important if you do not have to go under anesthesia, do not go. It is a dangerous place to be. Having surgery is dangerous, not because the doctor might kill you, but because your mind is now one blank sheet to be written upon by God knows what. I am not saying not to have surgery, but I am telling you that whenever you submit yourself to that knife and that gas, you ask God to keep your mind safe, preserve it, lock it away, keep it intact for when you re-enter this place called earth so that you might have it just the way you left it.

There are different kinds of souls. The underdeveloped soul: One that was never allowed expression of personality, its own individuality includes its wants, desires, opinions, or even needs. A soul that never got a chance to express itself. Babies born to crack addicts. People from lesser privileged zones and geographies. Deprived people, usually seeming to fall into a cycle of deprivation. Their souls never develop.

Fractured or wounded souls – about half of the church. One that is continually ridiculed, criticized, put down, punished for any expression, wants, desires, opinions, or needs. No wonder our kids grow up with a low self-esteem and turn to a life of crime, and we misconstrue it and label them as scum of the earth or a low life. We incarcerate, we punish, we penalize, we beat them down further. Go back just a little bit into their past and you will find that it was an underdeveloped, wounded, fractured soul.

An undisciplined soul. One that never has guidance or correction. For the person that has one, it is like having a very wayward, obnoxious, and rebellious thirteen year old. It needs restriction.

A spoiled soul. One that has been catered to all its life. Demanding, pushy, domineering, manipulative, whining when it does not get its own way. You need to introduce a word into that soul's vocabulary – "no". It needs to be denied. A super soul, one from which demonic strengths and forces are evident, needs deliverance.

VULNERABILITY TO DEMONIC HARASSMENT

Most often, if not all the time, it is sins of the heart that opens the door to destruction. Sin is twofold. Sin is an act and sin is a condition. I can commit a sinful act. I can also be a sinner, which is the present, continuous tense of the verb "to sin." Sin is an action verb. It is a doing or telling word.

I will never forget when I was learning verbs in elementary school. My teacher would drill in my head over and over again, "A verb is a doing or telling word." Then we had to go up to the front of the class and take turns to give a verb. I went up there to tell a verb and got to the front of the class, and I proudly pronounced "snake." My teacher got so mad. I remember him saying a bad word to me. My teacher cussed me. He used a real, real bad word to me because I made him so mad when I said snake was a verb. When he was able to calm down, he told me to go ahead and snake for them because a verb is doing and telling word. It dawned on me then.

You see the heart is the door to which we allow our lives to be structured or influenced. We commit acts of sin that are outward. Sins such as rape, murder, and stealing, are very obvious and outward sins committed as an act of sin. We can go to God because of this act of sin and can ask God's forgiveness and receive His forgiveness. Those are the obvious outward signs of sin.

SINS OF THE HEART

Unforgiveness is a sin of the heart. It is not an observable thing. It produces bitterness. It also produces judgement toward your family, friends and/or authorities. When we are talking about holiness and repair to the soul, there are three areas that are mainly affected and that is the area of rejection, resentment, and rebellion. When those three things take place, you then have unforgiveness.

Jesus has held that as a very strong and important criteria for the fulfillment and holiness of an individual. Look at what Jesus went through and He forgave them. Jesus says, "If you cannot do this one thing, forgive people, I cannot forgive you." I didn't say that; the Word of God says that. You tie his hands to forgive you.

What about bitterness? What about pride? What about anger? Animosity? What about rage? What about resentment? What about these things? These are conditions of our soul realm. We stay bitter. Bitterness is such an attitude it does not have to be outward. I can be so bitter to you without even laying a hand on you, inside of me I am jumping up and hitting you and you cannot feel it.

Bitterness resides within the heart it is not outward. These are open doors that we fail to pay any attention to. We want to kill the rapists and beat the burglars. In the meantime, however, while we are filled with righteous indignation and would love to kill the criminal, we kill our spouses daily because we have been with bitter with them so long. We are a little bit tired now and would like to have a newer version or an upgrade model. We think that that is no sin – you cannot see that. That is in your heart and as long as you can come to church and be nice and sit close to her, then I guess it is okay. Really and truly you think if God would take her home to glory, what a great spiritual thing that would be! Seriously though, it is the places of our hearts that opens the door of harassment and undue pressure and demonic activity.

Back in about 1998, I was really getting a little bit annoyed. I had been in a church and was the associate pastor and I had been there for about six or seven years. It was a great church, but somehow I started to get a little restless and I wanted to bust loose. It was time to get back out. My life had gone into disrepair and this man, who was my pastor, had nurtured me, brought me back to holiness, and helped me along. Now I was a little bit agitated and I wanted to do something. I had a few quarrels with him to go pastor at different places and he did not think it was right for me to go, and he was right, now as I look back. He did not think it was God's will for me to go. I started get a little bit agitated with him. The agitation grew and I started to complain, murmur, grumble, and become dissatisfied. Once I fed into that place and state of mind, nothing could please me. You could not do good on your best day.

When we get into that state, nothing pleases us. We find fault with God. When we cruise into criticism and we pick up the spirit of criticism, nothing pleases us. Nothing is good enough for us. Try as they may, people do their best to make us happy, and it is not good enough. I found fault with this man, a good man of God. All of the sudden, a man who had nurtured me from a state of disrepair when I wanted to have nothing to do with the ministry, poured into me, and now that I was strong, this was how I was repaying him.

All of a sudden, I got demonically oppressed, suicidal, and all kinds of things started happening to me. I was a crazed lunatic, literally. I got trained for what I am doing now under these very people because I had to go for deliverance. I was referred to a man of God. We were talking, and I know it was God because the secrets in my heart were too deep to share with anybody. I did not tell anybody I had it in for my pastor. I would be embarrassed to say that, so I know that I never mentioned it to a living soul. It was too embarrassing. It would be almost reproachful, ungrateful to go up against a man like that who had restored me, so I did not tell anyone.

I was talking to this man and telling him how I needed deliverance and how all these things were happening to me, and he said he needed to wait before the Lord. He then said, "This is what the Lord is saying to me. You have been complaining against your pastor. You have been murmuring, complaining, and grumbling against your pastor. You have broken fellowship with him in your heart and you are reaping the just reward from the Lord for going up against a man of God." This man did not know my pastor. He did not know me. I told no one what was in my heart. It was my secret, my sin, and he told it to me over the phone. When I hung up, I was fifty percent better immediately.

The spirit of criticism got hold of my heart and destroyed me. I went to him and we went through a series of things and I received tremendous inner healing, and then I trained under him. Criticism sapped the joy out of my life and took the marrow out of my bones, it seemed. It is a sin of the heart and it will destroy you, cause you to lose everything. I mean that physically. It seems like it starts with a stripping of your friends. All of a sudden, your friends do not want to come around you anymore. Then it creeps on to your job, maybe even until you lose it. You are just stripped bare. It is all pulled away and you are left naked before God. A critical heart is a terrible thing.

Another sin of the heart is jealousy. Not satisfied with what we have, the way God made us. Wanting to be made over. We want to challenge the Creator. We have an old saying back in Trinidad, "If problems were hung on a line, you would choose yours and I would choose mine." No matter how good it looks on the other side of the fence, you do not want my problems and I sure do not want yours. God forgive me for wanting to be like somebody else. Forgive me, Lord, for wanting me to be made over like Sister and Brother Perfect over there. We do not know what is working on the inside. We are not custom designed to carry that kind of load.

There is a true reflection in the natural world with regard carrying loads. We have Nissans, Toyota's, Fords , Dodges, Mazdas, etc.They are all built to carry the loads. We have ten-ton trucks and then we have U-Haul, and then we have trailers and combos. They are all designed to carry different kinds of payloads. We do not take a pickup truck and put a ten-ton load on it. It will crush the truck, ruin the engine. It just cannot handle it. We were designed carefully and wonderfully by God to carry a particular load.

"There hath no temptation taken you but such as is common to man: but God is faithful, who will not suffer you to be tempted above that ye

are able; but will with the temptation also make a way to escape, that ye may be able to bear it," I Corinthians 10:13

Your design is specific in the eyes of God. He will not burden you or cause you to be burdened beyond that which your frame can carry. So do not seek another person's burden by looking at them and thinking they have it together and you want that lifestyle. You may be so wrong. Choose what is yours. It is your mountain – climb it. Believe God for it.

Another sin of the heart is offense. People get offended for such silly things. The way we dress, the way we talk, the way we look, the way we comb our hair. People get offended at people they do not even know. We also take offenses by the things we hear.

Pride is at the root of denial. Blindness, stubbornness, no accountability.

TRAUMATIZED BEHAVIOR

Fear is the root of sin. The equal is not to trust in God. It comes out of wounding, desertion, or betrayal. One of the problems that I have found with fear in relationships as I have counseled, is people are usually traumatized by other people's behavior in relationships. Usually you do something that is really atrocious and it blows your mate apart. They become disoriented. They go into denial. Then they go into shock. Then they go into anger. You move through these phases.

Anger is not a really bad phase when you are coming out of trauma. It is your self searching for identity to return to your comfort zone and it is the way you express yourself. I encourage the clients that I counsel with to get in touch with their anger, because if they keep it a secret, it turns into bitterness. We need to get in touch with your anger. The Lord says, "Be angry and sin not," so I think He has given us permission to have an expression, but an expression without sin. If we do not do it that way, it will include sin and it will kill.

When we are traumatized, we do not rationally move away from trauma. We move away from trauma for safety's sake. For example, if I were to get struck with a pin, I would have immediate reaction. I would withdraw with great speed. I would receive an impulse and my brain would tell me to be away from the sources of the pain. That is what happens when a person gets hurt in relationships. Our spirit gets wounded and says to get away from the source of pain, and we go into withdrawal.

The process that will follow after, is a whole searching process where the spirit wants to come back to its comfort zone, so we may go through some denial, and we may go through some anger as a way of coming back. Some of the manifestations after withdrawal is a heart cry that says, "Can I come back? I want to come back to my place of comfort."

7

SINS OF THE FLESH

Immorality is a sin of the flesh. Transaction is another sin of the flesh – when you rip people off, you are dishonest with the scales, you adjust the figures, you add to the weights and measures, you cheat on the books, etc.

Control is an evil empire. You are forcing people against their will. Even though they are not saying no to you, you are psychologically manipulating them against their will. Domination, manipulation, and intimidation are all methods of control.

How do we respond to pressure? We are measured daily by the way we respond to situations. Our actions do not count for a hill of beans. It is our reaction that is the measure of our personality. We can do good all we want to do for the rest of our life and it seems like we are going unnoticed and no one will ever care. But respond to a situation in an unlikely manner and the whole measure of our personality and character is instantly judged, ostracized, and condemned.

How do you respond to pressure? Do you try to walk away? Do you try to reason and talk? Do I pray, "Oh God, take me out." Remember, the devil does not come directly at our spirit. He first has to get our mind overwhelmed, the area of our soul, the seat of our intellect, our wisdom, our rationale. Once he gets the place of our being confused, he can then invade or try to invade the area of our spirit and bring it into subjection.

The spirit is a divine mechanism in man whereby we can receive the divine of God and that is a sacred thing. I do not think it can be touched that easily. Our soul, however, is the area of problem. That is where we respond from. As one philosopher explains that there is an ability to have knowledge through the senses. I can hear, I can taste, I can smell, I can see. This is where I can find my knowledge coming in. This is the area that is usually subjected to the pressure of the enemy.

MODUS OPERANDI OF THE ENEMY

The enemy does not have any genuine, bona fide creative energies. The devil does not have the uniqueness and the originality of purpose. He takes everything that God has already made and alters its form in the life of a person who it leaning toward that persuasion. If we have an inclination, if we have a propensity toward evil it is so, even to be shaped accordingly. People of warfare like ourselves are trained in a particular way. Our systems are not bent backward, but we are bent forward. We are a people who are poised for battle. I made a film overseas a while ago. As we were driving the countryside along the coastline, we must have been driving for about eight miles through a coconut grove situated at the very edge of the country on the eastern side. The wind comes from the east and passes over and goes toward the west. All the coconut trees at the very front line of the shore, as it separates between the shore and the breaking waves, have all grown into the wind. It was a remarkable site. One looks at it and wonders with this constant force, this battering that is seeming to take place over and over twenty-four hours a day, three hundred and sixty-five days a year, endlessly, how come the limbs are not turned the other way and then pushed over.

As a matter of survival, even in the plant kingdom, in the ecology of the agricultural industry, and that was an agricultural area that we were going through, there is a law of resistance at work. As the pressures come on, these tender roots grow out into it, to equal its force and come above, and so grow in such a manner that they look like they want to fall down. The only thing that is keeping these trees from falling over into the ocean is the fact there is a consistent pressure against it keeping it up.

It is the very thing that comes against it that keeps it alive. It is the very work of the devil that keeps me going. If I have no force to contend with, if I have no enemy to contend with, a very real thing may happen. I may lay down and die, so to speak, spiritually. But because of the force that is against us as believes, we are trained to lean into it.

The devil does not create anything good. He is not a creator. He never has and he never will be creative. He is a perverter. He takes the works of God and finds feeble men who seek exaltation and works in the area of desire for exaltation, and perverts the true thing that God had created. He tries to be like God.

DOMINION VS. CONTROL

Dominion is a sacred word. The scripture teaches dominion. It teaches the ability to conquer, to rise up and take, to kill and eat and multiply.

It teaches dominion. The enemy perverts dominion and teaches control. There is a different between dominion that is godly, and control.

Control is ungodly and ruthless. Control has nothing about fairness involved in it. Control is pragmatic. Here I go on my philosophical rant again. The doctrine of pragmatism does not question the rightness or wrongness of anything. If something is workable, that is all it cares about. I will give you an example.

I do not always obey the speed limit. However, my point is this. Late at night when I am going home and it is about one or two in the morning, if I happen to be out at that time, and I am coming through the back streets heading home, and the traffic light is on red, I take a look to the left, a look to the right, in my rear view mirror to see if there are any bubbles behind me, and I go through the light. I am trying to show you what pragmatism, which is an element, a work of the devil, is. It says, "I am not getting into an accident. I am not hurting anyone. There are no cars around. I am not really putting myself out or anyone else. Why not go on through?" Pragmatism does not question whether something is right or wrong, it questions how workable it is.

The devil does not come to us and use logic about the rightness of any given sin. He has no interest in debating an issue with us as to its rightness. He only causes us to be consumed with how well this works for us. How much can we get away with? Pragmatism is one of the biggest forms of perversion that the devil has released upon the church. He says to the Christian, "Here is the Word of God. Now let's take a good look at it. On the one hand, we find a merciful and loving Savior, and within that plan, we find repentance, and just maybe if I do go wrong, I have at my disposal, repentance." So he settles the issue in our mind. Okay, there is room for us to mess up.

SLOW POISON

Once we arrive at the place, that there is room for us to mess up, the next thing he goes to is, "how much of this can we entertain?" How much of this can we take? How much poison can we drink before our system shuts down?

Now he begins to dilute the process of poisoning our system, a little drop at a time. Diffusion: the process of moving from one high point of concentration to a low point of concentration. By that I mean, just take a clear glass of water and drop one single drop of blue ink into it and watch the diffusion take place – moving from a high point concentration to a low point of concentration. In a matter of time, there is no blue about the water and to the onlooker and even the keenest eyes, there is still a certain measure of crystalline look about the glass of water. However, to the chemist, the properties have changed.

To God, the properties and the elements of our spirituality have changed. It has changed and we are not the same. We are tainted into compromise because of a pragmatic approach to the Word of God, the Kingdom of God, and this trial and error situation. He perverts that which God has given as the pure thing, the real thing. He seeks to corrupt, pervert, and change what God has ordained to be right.

What is right will remain right whether we had a rainy day or snowy blizzard. What is right is intrinsically right and will stay right, and the conditions of it being right do not depend on how we feel or any given situation. The Word of God is the Word of God, and it says the soul that sinneth shall surely die!

If you taint it just a little bit or a whole lot, the properties have changed. It takes the filtering of the Holy Spirit as we pour ourselves back into

Him to cleanse us again and put us back in right standing. So, the devil perverts. God has a blueprint; Satan has a perversion.

GODLY LOVE OR DEVILISH LUST

In worship, there is such joy in the presence of the Lord. There is such a sense of fulfillment and well-being. I love to worship the Lord. I love to lock myself in the car when I am driving and turn it up. I am worshipping God. I know people passing me by are thinking I am on something. Well, I am on something. I am high on the Holy Ghost and worshipping God in the beauty of holiness in the privacy of my sanctuary. And His love is surrounding me like a warm safe blanket.

There is something about love that puts it as one of the highest things in our lives, as to why we often seem to be defeated in that area. We are to share in the death and the baptism of death of our Lord Jesus Christ. It is love that killed Jesus. Greater love hath no man that this, that he lay down his life for his friends. It was love that took Him to the cross. It was love that crucified Him. It was love that caused Him to volunteer His soul up unto death and give up the ghost. It was love.

The devil seeks to take that very area – that very area of our Savior's death and resurrection, and His commitment to the cause of saving mankind – and he tries to pervert it. Love has turned to lust. The true love of God has turned to lust as it is perverted in the hearts of mankind. Let me get to the heart of the issue.

It is that desire in us that drives us to seek attention and to seek favor with man. At the very root of our foundation and of our being, stems a mechanism that says, "I want to be accepted. I want to be loved. I want a sense of well-being. I want a sense of purpose. I want to know you love me." We are overcome with it and there is a relentless pursuit so misguided, so misdirected, that it leaves the domain of love and all it becomes is a tool of conquering. Because of this thing I am talking about, we find ourselves in an effort to establish this relentless pursuit of acceptance and we pledge ourselves to loyalties that are ungodly.

We form ties, and bonds, and soul connections in an effort to say, "Love me." We do not need to love anyone so much to the point where we are controlled by that love and become a miserable, uncomfortable being because we are not measuring up to that love. Love is free. Love is of God. Love is not an entrapment. Men lust after women and create ungodly soul ties. Ungodly soul ties are a very real problem and is elaborated more in-depth in some of my other lectures and teachings , a simplified version is a basic three fold approach to how one makes or gets a soul tie , (1) through sexual contact in unsanctioned unholy situations (2) partaking of drugs or intoxicants that render one outside of the control of his or her mental faculties an impairment and allegiance to the spirit of the (pharmacia) original Greek word for pharmaceutical when translated means sorcery. (3) witchcraft, the willful or ignorant indulging in practices of the occult other methods of touching the dark side. That is the readers digest version abbreviated.

There is an immorality choking the life out of the church. There is an immorality in the secret places stifling the life out of us. It is a compromise of relationships with the opposite sex.

My name is Jeffrey Winston Leach. I am a part of the Leach family tree and line. My roots run all the way through England and Africa. I have a heritage. I have an inheritance because of this heritage. Everything connected to me in that line is what I call my personal luggage.

I had a grandfather who was a sorcerer. He would tell me stories of necromancy, of the power of evil when he would go to the cemetery and invoke the dead, and how it would come up with such tremendous roar and the graves would open and he would sit there and command them and give them assignments to go do his bidding. That is in my lineage. This is the stuff that generational and ancestral spirit and curses come down from to the decedents, these were real events and occasion from which I had to be delivered from with respect to ungodly soul ties.

With regards to a sexual ungodly soul tie, "Marriage is honorable in all and the bed is undefiled" (Heb 13:4.) Marriage prior to sexual intercourse is the only spiritual and legal force with the ability to cancel or avoid that. When you are unmarried and you do not have the blessing, and sanction, and union of God to copulate with another individual, you have no ability to break-off that generational, ancestral line. So when you, John Q. Public, go join with Mary Sue Public and interact sinfully, you have brought the whole heritage and lineage and baggage of your ancestral curses and line into a relationship in where she has brought her baggage also. Joined together, the two of you have created a new ungodly, uncontrollable size of debt a matrix of sorts that you cannot satisfy its debts. That is an ungodly soul tie and the church is not aware of the sinfulness and the tremendous evil that they practice when they sinfully engage in lust or perversions.

You have no idea the irreparable damage you do to yourself and the kingdom of God when you go astray in the flesh. If I could say one thing that would mean anything to you, it would be, "Clean up your sex life. Stay away from ungodly relationships outside of marriage – before marriage and after marriage. It is a death. It is a cancer!" Paul says, you hurt your own body when you do it, and he was talking about this physical body and beyond that. You hurt your own body when you do that.

SALVATION BY PROXY

In the area of the gifts, the genuine articles is the Holy Spirit, fruit of the Spirit, and the pure works of God. I Corinthians 12:7-11 "Now to each one the manifestation of the Spirit is given for the common good. To one there is given through the Spirit the message of wisdom, to another the message of knowledge by means of the same Spirit, to another faith by same Spirit, to another gifts of healing by that one Spirit, to another speaking in different kinds of tongues, and to still another the interpretation of tongues. All these are the work of one and the same Spirit, and He gives them to each one, just as He determines."

This is the genuine article from the Spirit of God, but the devil comes and he perverts it. He brings it into question. How about a little good luck charm? Make it look holy. Make it look connected. Even let it say something about God.

I met a young man the other day and gave him a ride. He was in the vehicle with me and I was trying to witness to him right away as he jumped in. He kept fidgeting and finally he found what he was looking for. He pulled this little card out and it had a picture of the blessed holy mother, . He said, "I keep this with me for protection."

I said, "What is it?" I looked at it and it said something about

Magdalene.

He answered, "I do not know."

I asked, "Why are you keeping it?"

Responding, he said, "Well, my mother gave it to me."

I pushed, "What does it mean to you?"

"I do not know, man, it is just supposed to bring me good luck!" He said defensively.

Somewhere in the writing on that paper had something to do with God, but not as the Supreme Being. As the son of a woman who is possessing more power than the SON himself is. I tried not to be offensive to him, but to say, "Come out from this darkness.

There is a truth of God that says there is one Spirit and this one Spirit flowing from it is the gift of healing, miracles, talking in tongues, and all the other things we just read. However, there is perversion that says we should have a good luck charm and some lucky bead or something like that.

Even the children of Israel got so blinded and so far behind in I Samuel 4:1-9, they had gone away from God. They were not in touch with God. They had just drifted away from the presence of God and now the Philistines were coming to get them. They felt the assurance by proxy. In other words, we know somebody who is good with God. Someone is walking around really proud and pompous because her mother is born again and spiritual, Holy Ghost baptized, and speaking in tongues, so by proxy of the relationship, she is okay.

I have never seen anywhere in the Bible where it said God had grandchildren. Your mother might be a child of God, a son or a daughter, but you certainly are no grandson because in the kingdom there are only sons and daughters.

Israel was feeling self-assured because of the proxy of the relationship. Then when the Philistines came up against them and they went up with their pompous attitude and faced the Philistines, the Philistines whipped them soundly, Israel had a flogging like they had never anticipated. They ran back home and started crying to God, "Why did you do this to us?" They brought the elders together. They brought the holy people, the proxy people who were supposed to be in touch with God. They complained, "God, why have you done this to me?" Then they said, almost like a good luck charm, "I know what it is. Let's go get the ark of the covenant that we left up in Shiloh at the house of God. Let's go get the ark of the covenant and bring it here, and we will have the power and protection now"

What a tragedy when the forces of darkness have no respect for you. When they brought the good luck charm into the camp, Israel had a celebration. They were rejoicing – the good luck charm had arrived. The Philistines heard it and said, "What has happened. A God must have come amongst them." For a fleeting moment, they trembled, but they overcame their fear and the Philistines said, "Men, stand your ground. Quit yourselves and be like men. Let's go up and take these Hebrew people lest they ensnare us and put is back in bondage."

The outcome of that is Eli's two sons got killed, Eli fell backward and broke his neck, his daughter-in-law gave birth to a son and they called him Ichabod. The glory had departed. What a tragedy when you reach for your good luck charm, and the enemy says, "I'm not afraid of you." Even if you call your good luck charm, "the ark of the covenant of God", if you are not living right, even if salvation is yours the enemy is not afraid of you. When we are living right, we can access the power of God. We can sing like the songwriter.

"It is mine, mine, blessed be His name. Mine for all eternity. It is mine, it is mine."

Be fearless, be ruthless, but be that way in the power of the Holy Ghost. That is deliverance.

WHOSE ON THE HOME THRONE?

The positions in the home are perverted. I encourage the men not to be tyrants, but to love their wives and their family. Not to be whining, wimpy men and send them outside in the cold to pick up the newspaper. Do what you are supposed to do. I almost feel there is a law in my house that I have to take out garbage. My wife will never take out garbage. That is the manly thing to do. I take out the stinky stuff. There are some things I just do, because it is the manly thing to do.

The danger of what I am trying to say is, avoid abdicating your throne. A lot of us have caused our wives to turn into manipulative, controlling agents because we failed to fulfill our responsibility, and our wives could do nothing else had no other choice but to assume the responsibility of where we abdicated. It had to be done, so she took up and did it. Even as she is doing, it is not the right thing, but we have caused her to be there. It is our fault and God holds us accountable for it.

Even if she innocently found herself usurping the authority and becoming what we want to call a Jezebel, we are responsible because we abdicated our throne and she did not have any other choice but to take care of our business, and when she did, she became a manipulator. We were the cause of giving birth to illegitimate authority.

Numbers 30 says, if your wife opens her mouth and decrees something before the Lord and it was wrong and you did not stop her, then whatever becomes of that consequence, you are responsible. Do not abdicate your throne. Do the right thing by your families, by your wife and your children. That is deliverance.

NECROMANCY

Acts 20:24 says,

"However, I consider my life worth nothing to me, if only I may finish the race and complete the task the Lord Jesus has given me – the task of testifying to the gospel of God's grace."

The grace of the Lord has been extended to us. We have to learn to accept the grace of God. One of the conditions for accepting the grace of God is to know right off from the very start, we do not merit it. That is what keeps us out and robs us. We walk around with self-pity and condemnation saying, "I am not worthy. I am not worthy." Well, okay, we are not. Settle the issue. We are not, but in spit of that God says, "My grace is sufficient for you" and "whom the son sets free is free indeed."

When you live your life constantly reaching back into the past, into the dead, old, rotten past of your life, there is a word for that. It is called necromancy – playing with the dead. When you mess with your dead past, it is necromancy.

When you cannot let yourself walk in the grace of God because you think you are so vile and so corrupt, and you had a horrible past, you are in necromancy, playing with the dead, walking in company with the dead!

Paul cries out and says, "Oh wretched man that I am. Who shall deliver me from this body of death?" There was a sentence in Greco-Roman history where prisoners who were condemned to die were strapped with the body of another dead person. He was set loose like that. That was his punishment. When that body began to decompose, it began to decompose the live body as well. Paul is making such a strong analogy. He says, "Who shall deliver me from this body of death?" He is alive, but he is tied with this big, huge hunk of death on him, and as that continues to rot, so goes him.

When you reach back and play with the dead, it is going to rot you as it continues to decompose. Let it go. Your past is your past. It is under the blood of Jesus Christ. He took it and threw it out into the ocean, and He put up a sign that says, "No fishing." Leave the past alone. Look forward to the future. Pressing to the mark of the high calling in Christ Jesus. Look forward. I do not care what you did.

8

DIRECTIONS TO DELIVERANCE

I like to think of myself as a street sign. Have you ever called someone on the phone and they said, "Tell me how to get there." You said go west on 20 until you see Green Oaks, then turn right on Green Oaks and go until you see Pleasant Ridge, and then turn left on Pleasant Ridge." They jump in the car and follow the signs. What a phenomenal mystery – they arrive at the right place!

The Word of God has signs. It says, "Turn ye not to the right. Turn ye not to the left, but go ye straight." There is a little voice giving you instructions as you make that move. He's telling you the way. "This is the way – walk ye in it. This is the way – walk ye in it and you will find rest for your soul!" That is deliverance. Follow the signs.

CONTROLLING THE SMALLEST MEMBER

There is a lady back home who had a problem with her husband. They were always quarreling. She went to the witch doctor in the village. She wanted a solution to her problem. He did not have to perform a trick or conjure up a spirit. He realized the woman had a problem repetitively purging herself thorough the mouth. He took a little water and dropped a little Kool-Aid in it and no sugar and shook it up. It turned red and he handed it to her and said, "Now listen women. Listen to me carefully. I want you to go home and when your husband comes home and you see him walk in the door, I want you to take a mouthful of this stuff. Do not drink it and do not spit it out. It is guaranteed to work every time."

She was ready for him. She had all the voodoo potion that she could ever get, some Kool-Aid and water, and as he walked in she put it in her mouth and held it. The guy went to bed and that was the end of the first night. The story repeats itself over and over. He was not only voodoo man, he was a conman and psychologist..... If we keep our mouth shut, we are going to stay out of trouble. That is the philosophy. If he told her to keep her mouth shut, she would have been offended at him probably slapped the man silly, so he gave her a potion to use. She used it and it worked or at least so she thought. We can save ourself a lot of headaches if we will control our tongue. The grace of God has come to us.

Ephesians 4:1-3 and 7 says,

"As a prisoner for the Lord, then, I urge you to live a life worthy of the calling you have received. Be completely humble and gentle; be patient, bearing with one another in love. Make every effort to keep the unity of the spirit through the bond of peace. But to each one of us grace has been given as Christ apportioned it."

There is a word there in that translation that I magnify out of the Greek. The word is eklektos. It is the selection process of God. It is like a man in a vineyard who discriminately picks the good and best fruit from the one that is not so good, to produce the best wine. To paraphrase the word and re-read it to you from the Greek into the English, this is what it says. "You are the selection of God. Guard your spirit to keep it in the bond of peace."

KEEP THE DOOR CLOSED, PLEASE!

Whenever you kick your pet outside, there is a constant, unending searching to regain entrance. He scours every door, every window, every port, every hole, and if possible, the air ducts and vents. He wants back in.

We have been discussing some really heard things in this text. Things sometimes so overwhelming that my own soul becomes fragile in the presence of God, because it is a lot to take and deal with. This mystery about heart purity is on the cutting edge of those who make it and those who do not.

We can all get in our cars and drive to a destination. Some will arrive in a Lexus, some in a Mercedes, some in a Dodge, and some in little a Ford Fiesta, but we will all get there. The difference in the ride on the journey is comfort, style, luxury, divine appointment, less stress, greater safety. I want to get there with great safety. I do not want my ride to be an ordinary ride. I want the divine appointment of the Holy Spirit. I want to live a cut above in my journey. That is what this is all about.

The goal of this text is to close the door to the enemy of our soul. I think it is fair to say that we have established and looked at several ways whereby we have opened those doors. We have delved into major subjective areas such as resentment, bitterness, impurities of thoughts and heart patterns, heart attitudes, and things like that.

It is so much easier to see the obvious and glaring and the things that stare us in the face because they come unto all mankind, such as overt crime, murder, theft, and those kinds of things, and so easy to miss the issues of the heart because they are not visible to the naked eye. They manifest themselves in fruits of behavioral patterns, but still go unnoticed because the roots have not been dealt with.

I have trusted the Spirit of God to bring forth those things that are necessary and applicable for life-changing patterns to help with dysfunctionalism in the spirit. At the seat of all this is increasing knowledge in the area of knowing who God is and who we are in Christ Jesus. To know is to be free because people perish for a lack of knowledge.

How would you like to know that you were in heir or heiress, that your dad or mom or whomever owns the largest bank in the nation? And all this time you had been living under a bridge settling for any kind of comfort you can take, facing the elements of all the harshness that life dishes out, and yet indeed you are wealthy beyond your wildest imagination. This is why we want to access – The wealth of God for us. Our Heavenly Father owns the cattle on a thousand hills and we are well endowed. We are rich.

UNMERITED FAVOR

How do we appropriate the grace of God? You must first understand the grace of God, which is the unmerited favor of God. It is something that you do not deserve and you get it anyway.

Anytime someone comes to me and they are in trouble or have a crisis and need prayer because their life hangs in the balance, a decision could be made that could send them completely into utter despair, I pray, "God, do not give them what they deserve." What you deserve is hell and destruction and death and utter ruin, but Jesus Christ left the splendor of Heaven of His own free will to come down to earth and to live and dwell among common man. To take upon Himself the sin of this world. Christ died for us even while we were yet sinners. He came to take our pain to the cross and a become substitute for us, because literally, when nails were driven through His hands and He was nailed to the cross, you should have been there, I should have been there. It should have been me! I sent Jesus to the cross long before He was ever crucified.

Even in the future, the sinfulness of mankind sent Jesus to the cross two thousand years ago. Therefore, for your unworthiness and my unworthiness, He took it upon Himself and He humbled Himself and became a man, and suffered death, agony, and torture so that you and I might go free.

I thank God that I woke up this morning, that I did not have a wreck and die, and I thank God that I am still in my right mind. I am not taking for granted that I am alive and breathing. I appropriate the grace of God. I should have been dead. I have committed atrocities in my life that were worthy of death and imprisonment, and God said, "You are free. You are clean by My blood and by My grace. You are free." I do not have to be crucified. I do not have to walk with the ugly baggage of my sin. I do not have to take the scorn of the world and live in constant guilt and rejection. I am free from the guilt and consequences of sin because Jesus Christ paid it all. The grace of God which came to me freely, purchased my salvation. For it was by grace that I am saved through faith in Christ Jesus. Not of any works by me, lest I should boast.

Ephesians 4:1-3 and 7

"I, therefore, the prisoner of the Lord, entreat you to walk in a manner worthy of the calling with which you have been called, with all humility and gentleness, with patience, showing forbearance to one another in love, being diligent to preserve the unity of the Spirit in the bond of peace. But to each one of us grace was given according to the measure of Christ's gift."

I challenge you to bear one another's burdens. I encourage you to make the load lighter. Take the responsibility to be united in the Spirit in the bond of love and peace.

We are the temple of the Lord and obedient to the alter in that temple. We need to be ready to lay on the alter anything that is not pleasing to the Father. We need to replace it with a faith-filled vision for Christ Jesus in us.

I Corinthians 6:19-20 says,

"Do you not know that your body is a temple of the Holy Spirit, who is in you, whom you have received from God? You are not your own; you were bought at a price. Therefore honor God with your body."

The problem with a living sacrifice is just that...it is alive. Live sacrifices have the tendency to get up and run. Dead sacrifices stay on the alter. Living sacrifices get up and run, so we have no real, genuine consecration because it is not crucified.

DO NOT REASON WITH THE DEVIL

After we have appropriated the grace for our lives, we have to learn how to walk yielded. Now I will try to explain to you a careful process of how one allows the doors to be opened, bearing in mind that we are talking about keeping the doors closed.

I told you before the devil does not immediately attack your spirit. He comes to the soulish area of your person and brings you into a place of compromise or reason. When he gets into the place of reason, then you have lost the battle. You cannot reason with the devil.

The devil then brings you into a place of compromise. Usually, he will not be obvious on what he is about to do in terms of showing you a blatant, graphic, layout of some kind of sin or some temptation. Usually people are wise enough not to submit themselves to real obvious temptations unless there is some kind of rare malady and they do not care.

Normally, though, it has to be a subtle poisoning of our mind. As I mentioned before, if you drop blue dye in water, one drop does not change the whole picture of the glass of water. It is diluted by the process of diffusion. It filters through and still looks clear eventually to the naked eyes, but to the eyes of the scientist in the lab, however, it is not the some thing. It has impurities, differences, color factors.

The devil will usually bring about some kind of doubt, such as when Eve was in the garden and being tempted. Eve knew the Word of God. God had given them the Word, told them what to do and what not to do. Satan comes and injects his subtle measures of doubts. He asks a question. ''Did God really say not to?''

How else can you get a man to reason unless you ask him a question? You are seeking his opinion on an issue. One of the key techniques to find out what is in a man's heart is to pose a question to him or pay him a compliment.

So the devil asks Eve, "Did God really say you wouldn't die?" Eve begins to question, "I guess I really need to consider this. Did He say that?" It opens the door for reasoning. Once you have opened the door for reasoning, you have lost. I have not seen a man who can reason with the devil. We are talking about a guy who has been here since the rock of Gibraltar was a pebble.

You have drifted away subtly from your original position, the things that you held to firmly, uncompromisingly. You gradually move from that place into a place of total compromise. In other words, the thought comes, and you begin to process the thought. Soon enough, you move to where the thought becomes overwhelming and you start to say to yourself, "I could survive this." Whenever you begin to think you can survive a temptation or survive an onslaught, or even worse than that, you begin to think that you can recover from it, your ship is sunk.

SIN AND RIGHTEOUSNESS ARE NOT COMPATIBLE

Remember there is a philosophy that says unity is strength. That is true in good or bad situations. If you do something long enough that is bad, you become strong in doing bad things. If you do something long enough that is good, you become good in doing the good things. Unity is strength in terms of how you put your forces together to do anything. It develops a pattern, a trait, a character, and attitude.

There comes a point of finality in terms of an individual being in logic with the devil where in order to commit a sinful act, he or she must dismiss the Holy Spirit from their lives. Up until you commit the act, you are forced by reason to consider the options of your actions. Up until then, you have not gone over. Sin and righteousness will not co-exist. There will not be a continuum in terms of sin and righteousness co-existing in the believer.

There comes a point in time when you rationally decide to dismiss the Holy Spirit. The subtlety of it is that you do not say, "Okay Holy Spirit, leave me alone." It is a thought process that says, "Okay I will do it," It is at that point in time you have dismissed and released the Spirit from within you, because up until then it is the Spirit that holds you together. It is the conviction of the Spirit that keeps you a whole person.

I am talking about a dangerous and detrimental process with regard to opening the doors to a tremendous, demonic kind of activity in your life. You invalidate the Holy Spirit's ticket. You must give Him reason or permission to leave because as long as He remains, you will not commit sin. You will hear a voice saying to you, "This is the way. Walk ye in it and you will find rest for your soul." Anytime you go beyond that, you say by your actions and by your reasoning, "Okay Holy Spirit, turn off for a little bit. Give me license to commit sin." That is a dangerous process. Do not ever get into reasoning with the devil. You cannot win when you reason with him.

The Bible says to resist the devil and he will flee from you. Do not talk with him, resist him. Treat him like the salesman you do not want calling at your door.

There is grace for your life, walking a yielded life in terms of not dismissing the Spirit in your life, and then there must be brokenness.

9

YOUR ACHILE'S HEEL

Genesis 22:8-14 is the story of Abraham and Isaac at Mount Moriah. Abraham had to take his son, Isaac, and place him on the altar and sacrifice him. You must understand that Isaac is the representation of the fulfillment of Abraham's entire life purpose. It was the seed in which the nations of the world would come, multitudinous to the extent of the sands of the seashore. It was the seed in which Jesus would eventually come down through. We are looking at a very significant, important issue in the life of Abraham.

Abraham was to take Isaac, the one possession, the one thing that could become the ultimate idol to Abraham, and sacrifice him on the altar. Isaac meant everything to him. It meant his marriage. It meant his relationship with his wife. It meant the future of the world as a result of having Ishmael. This was a very important issue in the life of Abraham. It was the one thing that could make or break him, and in many cases it did some of both. He was to take this one thing and put it on the altar.

What is in your life that could become a destructive force for you right now? I give an exercise for people with addictions to do. It is to write an essay about the one area of your life that has brought you into bondage. I have them write an essay or letter to themselves on all the trauma that could come about should they fail in that area.

You would be amazed at what shock therapy this is. It brings a rude awakening to the mass destruction we can cause because we are not people unto ourselves, we are interrelated by friends, family, generations, societies, businesses, by all kinds of means. We are an extension of something else that is pretty global in its perspective.

If you were to look through the invisible lines of connection that relate me to this world and people, it goes all the way to Africa. Therefore, the effect of falling into an entrapment and yielding to some kind of bondage stretches its tentacles and affects hundreds of people literally around you.

I ask them to write for me the destruction that can come about should they fail to make good on their ability not to succumb. They are amazed at the lives they will touch negatively.

Think for a while about the areas that have presented vulnerability to you. There is some kind of symmetry or pattern per se in an individual's life whereby he finds himself saying. "This is the one area I am afraid of." It is different for many people.

I like to work on strengths rather than weaknesses. I have no temptation at all for illegal drugs. They have no hold on me. Drugs have no hold at all on me. I would not lose one second of a night's sleep worrying about taking a hit of crack. However, there may be other areas that I am worried about, susceptible to, vulnerable to, and afraid of and must constantly keep my guard up. It is those areas that I am saying to you to put on the altar sacrifice and crucify it. Kill it! Put it there and let it move from your head to your heart, that it is dead, and the desires no longer exist.

Should it be anger, put it on the altar and say, "I am going to kill you today. You are crucified on the altar. You have no life within me. You cannot be resurrected." Consciously, spiritually, grab hold of the area of vulnerability and put it on the altar and say, "God, this is the area of my life that will affect generations and relationships and people in a most negative way, and God, I cannot and do not want to bear the consequences of my vulnerability should I slip and thereby affect the lives of so many people." Put it on the altar. Close the door.

We cannot afford to be people who are vague anymore. We must be specific. The devil is not vague and you cannot afford to be vague. Stretch deep within the recesses of your heart and mind and find those areas that present entrapment, and put them on the altar one by one and spiritually stay there until they have suffocated and drowned in the blood of Jesus Christ. Plead the blood of Jesus Christ upon them and say, "You die in the rich, red, crimson blood of Jesus. I suffocate you to death in the blood of Jesus Christ!" Not only will it die, but in the blood of Jesus Christ, it is sealed. That is important because when you seal it, even if it wants to raise its ugly head, the blood seals it and it cannot communicate with a cohort spirit to present problems.

There is a networking in the enemy's kingdom, and you might silence a spirit in your life, and it might be neutralized, but I have seen over and over again that even though a spirit is neutralized, he will surely reach out and communicate with another spirit that can carry the work on. That is why I seal things in the blood of Jesus Christ. Cut the communication link off, seal it, drown it in the blood of Jesus.

I have found in my work how groups of spirit families work. I may cast a spirit of bitterness out of you. That is just the supervisor spirit operating. He has working with him, anger, envy, strife, murder, malice, jealousy, hatred, violence, etc. We call him bitterness, but he does not work by himself. That is the ultimate effect, but he does not work by himself. When I kill bitterness, I seal it in the blood so he will not talk to anger, violence, murder, strife, enmity, jealousy. Seal off their communication network, because they talk.

Learn to do a complete work when you put it on the altar. It is dead and all its' ugly tentacles are dead with it. Look for the varying manifestations of the vulnerability. What happens when you become angry? You might have fits of rage. Then you do not just put anger on the alter...put fits of rage on the altar, too. When you become angry, do you become violent? Then do not just put anger on the altar, also put violence on the altar, too.

Put it all on the altar and crucify it. Kill it and stay there long enough to see it dead and make a conscious deliberation within your heart and mind that you will not pick it up again, because it is dead. There is a spiritual practice known throughout the ages and through the scripture called necromancy.

Necromancy, as I want to reiterate, simply means contacting the dead, conjuring up dead spirits, seeking and entrance into the realm of the spirit and the supernatural. Its' communication is based on getting in touch with the dead. It is energized from the dead, the past.

When you put that thing on the altar and crucify, and you reach back and touch that dead thing, you are into necromancy. You are touching base with the dead. That is spiritual witchcraft. When it is dead, it is dead. Leave it dead and do not go back after it. I do not care how you are tempted or what situation you are in to regurgitate the past and pull it back to throw in someone's face. It is dead and you do not touch it. It is spiritual wickedness to touch the dead. This will help a lot of people who need to realize what evil is being done when they grab something out of the grave of their past, pull it up, and bring it into their present situation.

Paul said, "Who shall deliver me from this body of death?" That was a living analogy of a form of death, punishment, or sentence in Roman history and culture . A man sentenced to death had several ways that he could die. Jesus was not the first one to be crucified. Crucifixion was a form of Roman punishment. That was just one way they could kill you'

Another way was to take you and strap a dead body to your back. That was what Paul was talking about. He was making an analogy of the depth of sin and he used a living Roman custom to make it. "Who shall deliver me from this body of death?" He was really trying to force the message home. They would take a dead body and strap it to your back and set you free. That was your punishment. When a dead body decays, it infects the living host body on which it is strapped, which then begins to rot the living body, and ultimately kills it. It is a horrible form of death. It is a slow, demeaning, horrifying form of death. You are living with death while you live looking forward to your death.

When Paul says, "Who shall deliver me from this body of death, oh wretched man that I am." He was literally using a live Roman historical analogy of punishment to bring home a spiritual message to people that the dead kills the living and to reach back into it and bring it back, is to bring punishment on you that is deadly. Leave the past alone. It hurts in ways you cannot even begin to think.

We have all had pasts. We have all done horrific things. We must leave the past alone and walk away from it. This is a brand new day. This is a brand new hour for the child of God, for the church of Jesus Christ, for the saints, the blood-washed, the redeemed. Nothing behind you is of great importance, except that it must serve as a reminder to not go that way anymore. Your future is before you.

In order to close the doors and keep them closed, you must take the authority of Jesus Christ to act in His name. He gave a great commission in Matthew 28:18-20, and the great commission is to go out and teach, baptize, and heal.

Jesus had a threefold ministry and implied it in the great commission to go do this is that threefold ministry. He told us to heal, teach, and cast out demons. That is His ministry to you. He gave authority and power. He authorized it and said, "Go do these things: heal, teach, and cast out." Take the authority of Jesus implied in the great commission. As you continue to close the door, apply that which has been given to you by the authority of Jesus himself and do the works of Jesus.

Lay hands and heal the sick through the power of God in you. Teach the Word of God, bringing men from darkness to light. The greatest miracle is still not getting healed from your cancer, or your heart disease. The greatest miracle is still being saved and brought from darkness to light.

The ability to see an individual in absolute darkness transformed into light is still the greatest miracle. To change by the renewing of your mind, old life patterns and to accept new life skills and ways through Jesus Christ.

Jesus commands us with His authority to bind the strong man.

Matthew 12:29,

"Or how can anyone enter the strong man's house and carry off his property, unless he first binds the strong man? And then he will plunder his house."

Mathew 18:18,

"Truly I say to you, whatever you shall bind on earth shall be bound in Heaven; and whatever you loose on earth shall be loosed in Heaven."

By Jesus' authority, He gives us the ability to break the curse of the law, and to reverse the curse.

One specific curse mentioned in this text was the one found in Deuteronomy 23:2, the curse of bastard, even though it is serious and severe we have through Jesus Christ the ability to break the curse of the bastard (the illegitimate or fatherless child) from ourselves and our offspring. We are no longer fatherless we are sons and daughters.

If you look at Deuteronomy 28, several verses therein.

It talks about the curses of the law. Remember, to live outside of the Spirit is to automatically embrace the consequences of the law. The Spirit gives protection, as we find in Galatians 3:13, "that Jesus became the curse for us and redeemed us from the curse of the law". If we are not under the redemptive covering of Jesus Christ in the Spirit, we automatically appropriate the law and the consequences of the law.

He gives us the authority to reverse the curse of the law. He gives us authority to use weapons, "for our weapons are not carnal, but mighty to the pulling down of strongholds." We have the authority to choose to obey the Word, Luke 7:1-10. We have the authority to be armed and expect to defeat the enemy, Ephesians 6:10-18 and Joshua 10:24-25. He gives us the authority to know who we are, to have self-identity in Christ Jesus. One of the most powerful weapons of warfare is to know who you are in Christ Jesus.

If you do not understand your heritage, your lineage of the family to whom you belong, you are a defeated person. However, when you know who you are in Christ Jesus, confidence emerges, confidence rises, and there is a boldness that comes. There is a sense of an indestructible man, an indomitable spirit. A sense that you are Christ's possession. You are blood-washed! You are Holy Ghost baptized! You are paid for with a ransom of the precious blood of Jesus Christ! You have His grace and unmerited favor! You are who you are because He chose to give you meaning, and being, and purpose, and because of that knowledge, you know that come what may, the devil is a defeated foe!

I recently had a revelation from God. For the first time, I understood something I have always said. I have sung it over and over again. "The victory is ours; the battle is the Lord's. So lift up your banner of praise." God showed me something about the victory being ours.

The analogy that He brought was really ridiculous – the Dallas Cowboys. I asked God how that made sense. He said, "Well you rooted for them years ago and they won the Super Bowl back to back in the nineties on both occasions. You jumped in your car and you drove down the street with an air of pride. 'Go Cowboys! Go Cowboys! We won! We won!" Then the Lord said, "You never even caught a pigskin. You never even kicked a ball. You do not even know the rules of the game and yet you are saying 'we won'."

Then the revelation started to get clearer. He says, "You were shouting the victory is yours, but the battle was the Cowboys', and you were lifting a banner of praise. You did not play; they played. You did not win; they won. They won for the state of Texas and that is where you were living at that time; Jesus fought! Jesus won! The battle is Lord's. The victory is yours. Lift up a banner of praise! He won it for you. I sat there and, man, did I have a riot in my soul! I never fought the battle, but I claimed a victory because I am Heaven bound and my team won! I shout to the mountaintops, "The victory is ours!" Jesus won the victory.

Made in the USA
Middletown, DE
14 May 2021